Praise

'If you want to lose weight, there comes a day when you need to look in the mirror and admit you're carrying a little too much "around the middle." Strategy is no different. If you've reached the point where you recognise a lack of it in your own life or business, then Charlie, through this book, steps in as coach, advisor, mentor and guide. He doesn't just tell you what to do; he shows you how to listen, communicate and act with purpose.'
— **Andy Yeoman**, Entrepreneur, Investor and reformed reluctant strategist

'If only Charlie's book had been written fifty years ago! Where was my strategy? Professionally and personally? Like most people in those days, I fear we just made it up as we went along. Charlie has taught thousands how to "do strategy." And crucially his advice isn't about theories and visions. It's practical and aimed at you and me, not just at "top people." Try Chapter Four on being a good listener, that rarity in public and private life. I recommend it. Yes, a book to change your life.'
— **David Davies OBE**, Broadcaster, BBC Journalist, former Executive Director of The FA, Government Advisor on Sport and Media.

'"I'm so busy". Ever feel or say that? But busy in service of what? Do you feel like you are eternally firefighting and chasing your tail? How can we get where we want to be, or even know where we want to be if we don't have time to take a breath? Good strategy has the power to help you define where you want to be and how to get there. But strategy is mysterious and the purview of only the top of organisations or brightest of us, right? This is what we are told. No longer. This book not only demystifies strategy, it codifies it into accessible, achievable, practical and simple steps. It's gives us examples and activities we can relate to and simply conduct. These will help us build a strategy that works, gets our heads out of the weeds, extinguishes the fires and sets us free to achieve our goals. An essential read for anyone wishing to elevate themselves from the eternal "too busy firefighter."'

— **LCDR Dickie Farrelly**, Leadership Coach, Royal Australian Navy

'This book brilliantly breaks down the mythical mindset of being strategic into simple, practical, steps. It combines rigorous theory and inspiring stories with humorous insights and real-world advice, from 80/20 decision making to unlocking creativity by going for a walk. A must-read for anyone who's ever been told to be more strategic but has no idea where to start.'

— **John Sills**, Author of *The Human Experience*; Managing Partner of The Foundation

'*Be More Strategic* is a gem. It makes strategy accessible and attainable for everyone. It is a practical guide that demystifies and neatly knits together the

multiple facets of useful strategy. The anecdotes and references make it an enjoyable read too. Enjoy.'
— **James Alexander MBE**, Co-founder and former Executive Director of Zopa; Strategy Director at Egg; Chair of Finance Earth, Agricarbon and Suffolk Wildlife Trust; Trustee of RSPB

'I'm not a prolific reader of theory and if I don't enjoy something, I put it down quickly. This book hooked me from the start. It's engaging, refreshingly personal and full of practical tools that made me highlight, scribble notes and jump back and forth through the pages like it was a workbook. The blend of stories from business, sport and science keeps it relatable, while the exercises and clear frameworks make strategy feel personal and achievable. It's the rare kind of book that makes you think deeply about yourself, your work and how you lead – all while keeping it simple, compelling and actionable.'
— **Tim White**, former Chief Strategy Officer, Corporate Executive Officer and EVP at Fujitsu

'I wish I had read this book when I was in a number of senior, transformational roles – it would have made me more cognizant of what strategy deployment actually is, made me aware of my strengths, ability to influence and avoided a number of painful lessons!!
'I found the book very insightful and it gave great examples and insights of how you deploy a strategic

plan in a pragmatic way and successful manner, underpinned by a cohesive high performance team.'
   — **Geoff Cousins**, former CFO North America and MD Jaguar UK at JLR, Chairman of G&P Quality Management, Chairman of Cure Leukaemia

'If you want to be more strategic, from whatever level you believe you are at now, this book is an excellent place to start. The twelve practices are presented in a well-researched and accessible way and will equip you with a practical framework to build your skills and capabilities. The book presents a unique combination of theory, real-world case studies and individual exercises to bring to life how we can all improve our approach to strategic thinking, both in the business world and in our personal lives.'
   — **Steve Brandon**, former Partner and Board Member at Deloitte UK LLP, Non-Executive Director and Board Advisor, angel investor

'Meet Charlie, who I'm now calling my new strategic guru. He's spent decades watching people squirm in boardrooms when their boss says "be more strategic" – because, let's face it, half the time the boss like me, doesn't know what that means either! Charlie, in this book, helps us crack the code on why we all nod knowingly at strategy presentations while secretly feeling completely lost, and it turns out the culprit is our collective confusion between strategy (the scary stuff about making hard choices and dealing with complexity) and planning (the comforting world of to-do lists and organised meetings). Through his twelve practical techniques (that even a knackered old rugby player like me can understand), this book transforms strategy from an elite corporate mystery into something you can actually use – whether you're navigating office politics or figuring out your life direction. The best part? The author proves that strategic thinking isn't just for offices and CEOs through sharing stories of clients who've applied these same principles to buy castles, strengthen relationships and generally stop stumbling through life hoping things work out. It's like having a wise mentor who finally explains why you're beautifully organised plans sometimes lead nowhere, and shows you how to think bigger, choose smarter and actually build the life you want instead of just planning for it. I will absolutely be recommending this book to my clients.'

— **Lewis Moody MBE**, 2003 Rugby World Cup Winner, Performance Coach, Haddon Coaching

'Quite simply one of the best business books I've ever read. Should be on the desk of every CEO. Charlie Curson has managed to write a Rolls Royce of a business book. Each chapter is perfectly engineered, easy to follow and clearly comes from years of practice and research. But what I really loved is it's not just a strategy for business but for LIFE. I will be getting my kids copies and telling them, "You want a guide for life – it's all there!" It's also such an easy read, each chapter a step-by-step guide to putting together the ultimate killer strategy – but at the same time packed with insights, wisdom and practical "how to's." I suspect in a few years' time it might end up being one of those, "Read these three books young un' and you'll be sorted for life."'

— **Jack Milner**, Comedian, Playwright and Improvisation Specialist

'Businesses and leadership need this book. Why? Knowing Charlie personally, the read was like hearing his voice; a friendly talk – authentic, true, conversation-like.

'Providing wisdom and experience while staying informal, all supported by facts, cases, research, reflective questions, takeaways and actions makes it unputdownable, simply a page-turner.

'You want to "Be Strategic?" This is a map – the invitation for a trip with four stops and twelve road signs, and includes a backpack of author's wisdom, experience, tools and his nexialist partnership towards a progressive trip to seeing wide and true.

'It's a journey from self-awareness, through social skills and mindsets, courage and acceptance, striving to scale your impact.

'The big picture book, with a big picture map and deep-dive moments on each important road sign.'

— **Piotr Jankowski**, Founder CoachMentor. Team, Executive Coach PCC ICF, Leadership Mentor and Strategic Consultant, Ex Managing Director and Board Member Fujitsu Poland

CHARLIE CURSON

BE MORE STRATEGIC

12 ESSENTIAL PRACTICES TO BUILD THE LIFE AND CAREER YOU WANT

R^ethink

First published in Great Britain in 2025
by Rethink Press (www.rethinkpress.com)

© Copyright Charlie Curson

All rights reserved. No part of this publication may be reproduced, stored in or introduced into a retrieval system, or transmitted, in any form, or by any means (electronic, mechanical, photocopying, recording or otherwise) without the prior written permission of the publisher.

The right of Charlie Curson to be identified as the author of this work has been asserted by him in accordance with the Copyright, Designs and Patents Act 1988.

This book is sold subject to the condition that it shall not, by way of trade or otherwise, be lent, resold, hired out, or otherwise circulated without the publisher's prior consent in any form of binding or cover other than that in which it is published and without a similar condition including this condition being imposed on the subsequent purchaser.

Cover design by Stuart Harris
Cover image © Shutterstock | Jozef Micic

For Evie – ever curious,
and for Freddie – ever creative.

Contents

Foreword

As you begin this book, you'll quickly discover that it is not just another business text about strategy. *Be More Strategic* is an engaging blend of practical advice, real-life reflections and relatable examples of how great leaders and teams think and act to succeed.

Charlie combines human-centred insights with personal growth ideas and, importantly, an accessible approach to strategic thinking. In many ways, it feels like having a highly experienced executive coach and trusted advisor sitting alongside you—distilled into these pages, ready to guide you in the moments that matter most.

What I found most compelling is its deeply human-centred approach. Too often strategy is discussed only in terms of models, processes and frameworks, or theories that are detached from the people who must live them. Charlie takes a very different path. While he does reference some frameworks and models, the book's real gift is how it demystifies and simplifies what it means to be more strategic and less operational – a shift I continually see lacking in leadership teams. Just as importantly, it reminds us of something often overlooked: the essential work of leading beings with the work we do on ourselves.

The emphasis here on self-awareness and emotional regulation is both refreshing and essential. Charlie validates that the way we show up as leaders—calm, present, emotionally regulated—can have an enormous impact on the outcomes we create. For me, this was a joy to read because it resonated so deeply with my own work with leaders and their teams. It also speaks to what I believe is sadly missing from so many boardrooms today – yet could so easily be improved, unlocking far greater performance for teams and organisations alike.

The depth of research underpinning the book is impressive. Charlie has brought together strong academic referencing with vivid evidence from his own work across an eclectic mix of leaders, cultures and sectors. This gives the book both rigour and richness. And yet, despite its grounding in research and experience, it never feels heavy or inaccessible. Quite the opposite—it is engaging, clear and easy to stay with. In fact, I tested it by listening to the book, and it held my attention from start to finish. That is rare for strategy or leadership texts, which often fail to maintain that kind of engagement. The fact that this one does speaks volumes about Charlie's clarity of thought and his ability to translate complex ideas into compelling, practical guidance.

As an Executive Coach and Board Advisor, having spent much of my career in global senior leadership roles, I know how often leaders and teams find themselves caught in the operational weeds— working harder and faster, but not necessarily with more impact. The gift of this book is that it creates the space and perspective leaders need to rise above the noise. It offers exactly what today's fast-moving and often chaotic world demands: clarity, humanity and a practical way to think and act more strategically.

It is both a guide and a provocation, encouraging you not only to think differently but to *be* different.

My encouragement to you, as the reader, is not to treat these pages as theory, but as an invitation. An invitation to pause, to reflect, to experiment and to grow. What you will find here is not simply a toolkit for strategy, but a guide for leading with greater intention and humanity.

So, take your time with this book. Allow yourself to sit with its ideas and test them in your own world. If you do, I believe you will find that Charlie has given you something rare: a work that is both intellectually rigorous and deeply practical; both strategic and human. And in that, he offers exactly what many leaders are seeking today: a rare combination of clarity, wisdom and humanity. I cannot recommend this book highly enough.

Julie David, Executive Coach and Board Advisor; former Senior Leader in the global automotive industry for companies including Stellantis, Jaguar Land Rover, Volkswagen Group and Ford Motor Company

Introduction

Winners, in business and in life, are *strategic*. Being strategic is a game changer, in your personal life as much as in your professional one. People who are strategic are far more high-performing, happy and fulfilled.

This isn't another book on strategy. It's about being strategic, and the benefits that brings.

Would you like to have more impact as a leader and decision maker? As a human being? Do you struggle with making bold decisions, seeing the big picture, thinking long term or hearing alternative viewpoints?

Has your boss ever told you to be more strategic, but you don't know what that means (and, you suspect, neither do they)? Have you sat through presentations about the strategy for your team or organisation – death by PowerPoint – that leave you feeling confused, alienated and anything but engaged and motivated? Worse, have you given such a presentation?

You are not alone, but help is at hand.

Strategy itself is so misunderstood. The problem is, learning how to 'do strategy' seems rather secretive, hidden away in the upper echelons of corporations and business schools, making it not just mysterious, but also somewhat elitist and inaccessible. The requisite skills, knowledge, shift in mindset and respective behaviours are, for the vast majority, difficult to both access (cost effectively) and develop.

Strategic thinking or being strategic is widely perceived to be for the people at the top. Even at the top, though, it's often regarded as someone else's responsibility or, when you really push, it doesn't actually exist at all.

Within many organisations, rather than entire teams being involved in the important choices and decisions about their own future direction, the task is often handed to a single individual or specialist department, or outsourced entirely, possibly to those strange beasts called consultants. I am one of those consultants. I am also an experienced, qualified performance coach. Having taught thousands of people how to 'do strategy', I know that with a little guidance, anybody can be well set up to design, develop and execute a clear, robust strategy in a professional working capacity *and* in their personal lives.

The real key to winning in business and in life, to unlocking potential and having lasting impact is to be strategic. To be a strategic thinker and act, communicate and lead strategically.

Many people say that strategists have skills and characteristics such as analytical prowess, industry expertise and financial acumen. Others say that they are good strategic planners (whatever that means). That's only part of the picture – or possibly missing the point entirely.

Good strategists – and good strategic thinkers – do not think in isolation. They consider the big picture, the wide context, however complicated; they are able to zoom out (and back in again), operating at a macro level, scanning complex situations and landscapes, considering multiple potentially contradictory insights, trends and changes simultaneously. They spot patterns and gaps that others may miss. They sense-make.

They have good self-awareness. They recognise that their own choices, decisions and actions occur in a fluid, dynamic environment, one that also involves the choices, decisions and actions of many others. They foresee and/or anticipate the moves (and counter-moves) of others, and how everyone influences each other's choices, strategies and outcomes, creating opportunities as much as issues and threats. They balance the long-term strategy with the near-term tactical execution.

I have been privileged to work with thousands of people from many different cultures and backgrounds over the past few decades. In so doing, I have worked closely with a handful of people who always seem to be one step ahead, in life and in work.

These are people who are comfortable with uncertainty. They are good listeners, willing to make bold decisions often with limited information. They exude a quiet, considered confidence in everything they do. They balance being tactical with being strategic to optimise their effectiveness and the potential impact of their decisions and actions (or absence thereof). They embrace diversity and understand the value of seeking as many different viewpoints as possible. They own their mistakes as well as their wins, and are able to influence those around them to do the same.

If you adopt the practices explored in this book, this could be you.

As with any transformation, becoming a great strategist requires a paradigm shift in the way you think, act and behave, but it's learnable. I have two decades' experience in teaching people not only how to do it, but how to become it.

A long-standing client summed up the transformation a few years ago when he said to me, 'I want to be a bit more Yoda!' He's not using a light sabre yet, but he's become an exceptionally effective strategic leader through hard work, focus and a willingness to experiment and learn. This has paid dividends in his personal life, not just his professional one.

I've worked with another client, a serial entrepreneur, for more than ten years, as both a strategic advisor and a coach. Having created many strategies for his businesses to great effect, we decided to apply the same tools and techniques to his own life, which has had a profound impact on how he goes about his day-to-day. Stronger relationships, clearer mind, more balance and far more ambition are just a few of the benefits he's experienced. In fact, though he was loath to admit it, during one coaching session, it emerged that his real ambition in life was to buy and renovate a castle.

A few years later – he is now that person!

Who am I?

My career has comprised of three increasingly complementary activities – consulting, capability building and coaching. As a consultant, I have been involved in the design, development and execution of hundreds of strategies for teams and organisations all over the world, from global corporations to early stage start-ups, in almost every sector.

These strategies have been at an organisational level, but also divisional, functional, geographic and for products, channels and markets. I have focused on growth and innovation, on cost-cutting and survival, on international expansion and relocation, on mergers and acquisitions, and on fund-raising, pivots and exits.

While building capabilities, I have upskilled thousands of people – from experienced leaders and business owners to newly qualified graduates and everyone in between – not only to create their own strategy (and develop and execute a robust plan to deliver it), but also to think, act and communicate more strategically. As a qualified performance coach, I support managers and leaders and, in many cases, their leadership teams. Much of this is about helping people – and teams – to achieve their potential and get out of their own way.

My professional background is somewhat eclectic: an engineer by training, a career consultant (from technology to strategy-focused), a qualified performance coach, an experienced moderator and facilitator, an angel investor and scale-up advisor. I am what people might describe as a generalist – but with deep pockets of specialist knowledge and experience.

Through working with high-performing teams and coaches not just from business, but also from military and sporting backgrounds, I have learned about how the brain and body function, particularly under pressure, and the powerful effect of emotions on our behaviour. I am also a qualified neuro-linguistic programming (NLP) practitioner, which has taught me a lot about the way people think, feel and behave – including body language. My coaching career has led to me exploring and applying many powerful concepts relating to the inner game and the role of the unconscious mind.

I have coached many people who have developed into strong strategists, practitioners and leaders, each in their own unique way, each focusing on different skills, mindsets and behaviours. Working so closely with thousands of people all over the world has given me a unique perspective on how to unlock and develop the underpinning skills and attributes of being more strategic in individuals. Over twenty-five years, I have acquired a mass of tried-and-tested tools, techniques and examples that form the crux of *Be More Strategic* – all shaped around a powerful development framework and methodology.

Strategy isn't mysterious or reserved for the elite, it's a learnable skill, and it matters. Not just for leaders at the top, but for anyone who wants to make better choices and have more impact in work and life. I wrote this book out of frustration with the vagueness and inaccessibility of learning to be strategic, and to show what it really means, and how anyone can do it.

The twelve practices of strategic mastery

Anyone can learn to be more strategic and become a better strategic practitioner. The first step is to understand what this means in practice, and be able to assess your own skills, behaviours and competencies to create a practical, personalised development plan.

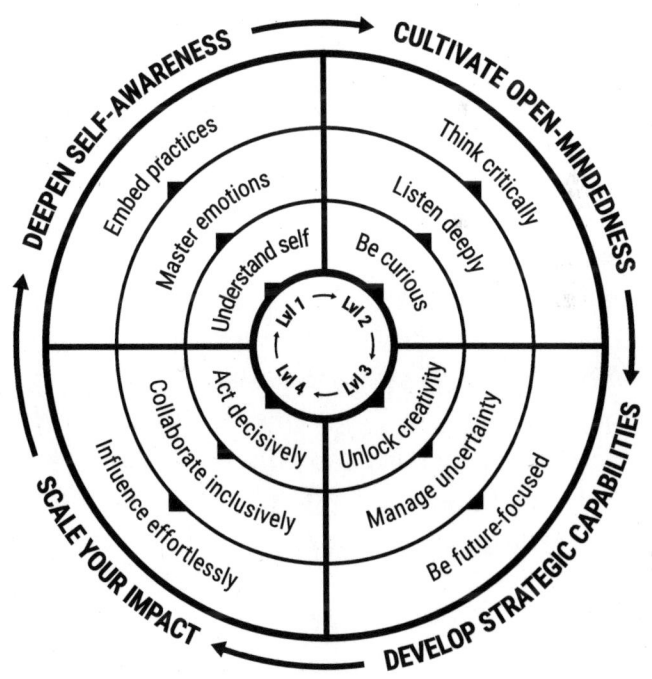

The twelve practices of strategic mastery start with building self-awareness, knowing your strengths and gaps, and recognising your triggers and biases. Self-awareness is the foundation of the framework, the key to vertical development (developing an evolving mindset and inner capability to handle complexity, ambiguity and change) as opposed to horizontal development (expanding your skillset or toolkit). To put it another way, the former is about how you think, the latter about what you know or can do.

Part One not only covers the foundation of self-awareness, it also outlines the traits of a strategist, the skills and knowledge, mindset and behaviours, and clarifies what the terms 'strategy' and 'strategic' actually mean. In Part Two, you'll learn to expand your thinking by staying curious, listening deeply and developing critical thinking skills. Part Three covers acting confidently through uncertainty, unlocking creativity and being future-focused. Finally, Part Four deals with scaling your strategic influence and leading with impact through bold decisions, harnessing diverse talents through collaboration, and communicating to inspire action, align stakeholders and make your strategy story compelling and persuasive.

The framework is progressive, so you can work through *Be More Strategic* from start to finish, using the supporting resources as required (QR codes at the end of each chapter will link you to my website), or dive into any chapter – any part of the framework – that captures your attention (eg be more creative, be more decisive). It's likely that you will then be drawn to read the earlier chapters.

To lead the life you really want, you will benefit from learning at least some of the 'secrets' taught in strategy school – but through the lens of someone who has applied these principles and practices, tools and techniques thousands of times in many different contexts and situations. *Be More Strategic* delivers all this, acting as much more than just a first step on the not-so-mysterious ladder to achieving more impact in your personal and professional life.

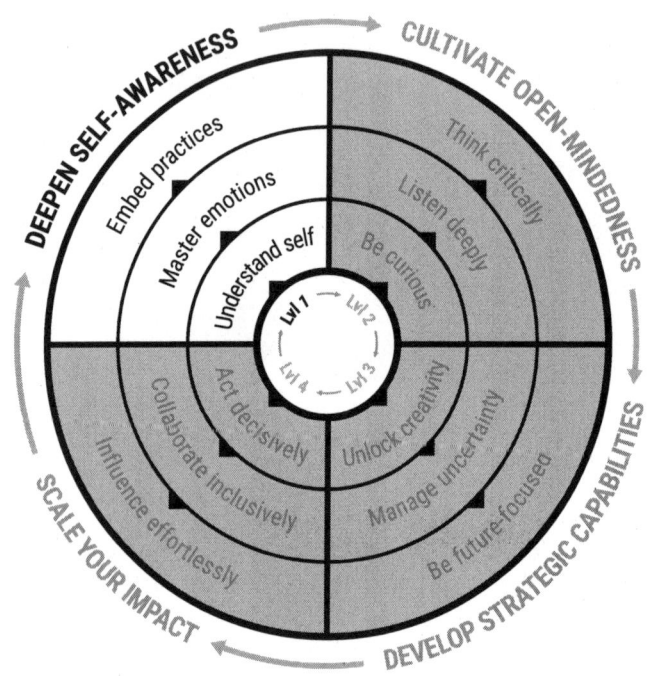

PART ONE
LEVEL 1 PRACTICES – DEEPEN SELF-AWARENESS

Strategic thinking is something of a superpower. Great strategists create as much as they critique. They identify challenges and spot potential opportunities. They confront problems and offer innovative solutions. They think deeply and act decisively.

The secrets of how to be a great strategist are hidden away in the ivory towers of corporations and academic institutions, saved for the intelligentsia. Are they really, though?

They're not actually secrets at all – they're just misunderstood. Everyone has the potential to be a great strategic thinker and a great strategist. Becoming one is easier than you might think.

Before we explore the traits of a great strategist – the skills and knowledge, the mindset and behaviours – let's clarify what we mean by the terms 'strategy' and 'strategic', and how these differ to planning.

1

What Being Strategic Means And Why It Matters

Let's start by defining strategy.

No one ever seems to agree on a single definition! Of the many famous definitions, these are some of the more useful:

- 'Strategy is about making choices, trade-offs; it's about deliberately choosing a different set of activities to deliver a unique mix of value.'[1] This is Michael Porter, revered in strategy circles, talking about competitive strategy in the 1990s.

- 'Strategy is a pattern in a stream of actions.'[2] This is management expert Henry Mintzberg's definition of emerging strategy from 1973. In the same article, he emphasises that strategy can be understood not only as a formal plan but also as emerging patterns in how decisions and actions unfold over time. I like the idea of patterns – and the mention of decisions. We'll explore both.

- 'Strategy is the art of war; it is about defeating the enemy without fighting.'[3] General Sun Tzu's definition from 5BC. I've learned more about strategy from diving into the world of philosophy and military leadership than I have from business. Give it a go!

People may not agree on the definition, but most agree on how important having a strategy is. Of those working in this field, past and present – Sun Tzu included, the majority agree that strategy is different to planning.

When working with a client on their strategy for the first time, I always treat getting clear on what they actually need vs what they think they need (or are expecting as an output) as a crucial initial step. Some may be bringing me in to help create or refine their strategy – possibly define their mission, vision or ambition too – and be very clear on what that means in practice. Some have a strategy – but aren't sure where it originated, or if it's any good, or if everyone knows and understands it. Some are asking for help to define their goals, targets, priorities and plans. Some are asking for help to improve the performance of their team or their own leadership style and approach. A few simply want me to rubber stamp their ideas – to act as external endorsement (or a human punch bag).

I regularly spend time upskilling leadership teams on what strategy really means, how valuable it is and, most importantly, how it differs to planning (we will examine this distinction later). It is not uncommon that a client initially says they need or want a strategy, but what they really need or want is a plan and clear set of priorities. If this happens to be a long-term plan, it might be upgraded to a strategic plan – but it's a plan all the same.

I should stress that having a good, robust plan is valuable. Of course it is, but it is different to having a clearly understood strategy.

Other clients discover that what they believed was their strategy, isn't a strategy at all. In fact, many start to realise that they don't have a strategy – certainly not a clearly communicated one – but quickly recognise the value of having one. We need to work on creating that before we define and agree the team's goals, targets, priorities and plans.

Interestingly, the same is true in our personal lives. In my experience, the highest performing and most fulfilled people have a clear life strategy. They have proactively applied the same strategic skills and mindset to define their life choices as they use in business, and have planned and executed accordingly. Having a personal life strategy – and being more strategic – are the keys to living the life we truly want.

A good strategy will recognise or acknowledge the most critical issue(s) or challenge(s), the one(s) preventing you from making progress towards your ambition and your ultimate objectives. It will set out how to deal with that issue or challenge, and what you need to prioritise. A good test as to whether or not you have a clear strategy is to try explaining it to someone. If their natural response is to ask, 'How?', you probably have work to do.

Richard Rumelt, the author of the excellent book *Good Strategy, Bad Strategy*, provides this brilliantly simple definition: 'a good strategy identifies critical challenges, leverages key strengths, and focuses resources coherently'.[4] Rumelt goes on to describe the events of the Battle of Trafalgar to illustrate effective strategy, explaining how Admiral Nelson faced a significant challenge – his fleet of twenty-seven was outnumbered by the thirty-three generally larger and more heavily armed Franco-Spanish ships. Nelson broke with naval convention by dividing his fleet into two columns and attacking perpendicularly, leveraging his fleet's superior seamanship and gunnery to great effect – and a famous victory.

Rumelt talks about a strategy having a kernel: diagnosis, a guiding policy and coherent actions. Nelson's abandonment of conventional line-of-battle tactics in favour of his own diagnosis, policy and action made all the difference.

Strategy or plan?

Many people I work with come from operational backgrounds and either recognise or are told at some point in their career that they need to be more strategic.

Nearly all of them – eventually – admit to not really knowing what this means. As it usually turns out, nor do many of the people who did the telling.

In explaining how strategy differs to planning, I often ask clients if they use to-do lists and for what reason. Reminders, reassurance, feeling organised? I then ask how they would feel at the end of a really good, productive planning meeting. Motivated, clear, excited, focused, confident?

Can you see the pattern?

Planning helps to lessen our feeling of anxiety. That's why creating a plan is a good first step in many health and wellbeing related practices.

Strategy is a completely different proposition. Managing complexity? Holding multiple paradoxes? Balancing the tension of logic and intuition? Ruling things out? Making tough choices? Even working out what all those choices and options are? These are all aspects of strategy that tend to make many people feel incredibly anxious.

Strategy is not a long shopping list of activities and initiatives. It is not financial projections and forecasts, and it certainly isn't hundreds of PowerPoint slides that nobody reads, let alone understands.

Your strategy may just come to you in a flash of inspiration, or when you're talking to a few friends or colleagues. It may take months to formulate. You can't say the same about planning.

This table sets out why strategy is different to planning.

Strategy vs planning

Strategy	Planning
Big picture view. It's about long-term positioning.	Sequential view. It's about short-term actions.
Sets the direction; connects intentions to outcomes.	Coordinates resources and tactics for effective execution.
What if...? Strategy explores alternative scenarios, embracing uncertainty and non-linearity.	What next...? Planning defines pathways, offering certainty and linearity.
Requires creativity; benefits from multiple diverse perspectives and insights.	Requires disciplined thinking; benefits from logical, well-structured processes.
Involves making hard choices and establishing priorities.	Involves taking a set of choices and mapping them into plans.
Seeks to influence what is beyond our direct control.	Seeks to provide a sense of control.
May increase anxiety.	May reduce anxiety.

Many people rush into planning without exploring or clarifying their strategy first. Then, partway through executing that plan, they start to wonder why they're not seeing the results they expected or having the impact they so desired.

If you think you're potentially developing or executing a plan rather than a strategy, you could do far worse than reflect on the brilliantly simple yet effective strategy choice cascade by Roger Martin, former Dean of the Rotman School of Management, as set out in *Playing to Win,* which he wrote with P&G's CEO, Alan George Lafley.[5]

You start the strategy choice cascade by asking yourself these questions:

- Have you defined your 'winning aspiration'?

- Have you defined 'where to play', ie where to allocate your resources?

- Have you defined 'how to win', ie how you will create value from your activities?

In fact, you can work through these three questions and iterate between them with a small team for a few hours to give you a far better sense of your strategy (or your strategic options). You'll notice that you haven't come close to a plan.

Now ask yourself:

- Have you identified your must-have capabilities to create maximum value and exploit your opportunities?

- Have you identified the systems required to build and maintain your advantage?

If you aren't exploring and answering these questions, Roger Martin says, you aren't developing or executing a strategy. There's much to explore and discuss about the five questions themselves – which Martin does in a Medium.com article.[6]

Strategy and planning might be different entities, but doing both properly, proactively connecting intentions to outcomes – now that's a powerful concept. People often ask me about the difference between being strategic and being tactical, and how tactics (and execution) differ from strategy (and planning). Though there are many ways people choose to define these terms, there is no one finite answer to either question. My own personal take would be this.

If strategy is about making unique choices that define a clear direction and provide a guiding framework for decision making, and planning is the process of organising tasks and resources against specific timeframes to achieve particular goals, then tactics (and execution) are where the work happens. They're where the effort is, implementing those plans to achieve those strategic objectives, aligning actions with intended outcomes, and ultimately making the vision – or 'winning aspiration' – become a reality.

In fact, tactics are arguably the most near-term actions, those based on the most certainty. They might at times appear completely at odds with the longer-term strategy.

For example, in Airbnb's early days, the co-founders sold limited edition cereal boxes to generate some much-needed cash flow.[7] It was around the time of the 2008 US election, and the cereal boxes featured Barack Obama and John McCain. These near-term tactics – a good example of bootstrapping – generated revenues of more than $30,000, helping the business to survive long enough to execute its strategy.

This 'tactic' also impressed Paul Graham, the founder of start-up accelerator Y Combinator, who said, 'Well, if you can convince people to pay $40 for

$4 boxes of cereal, maybe, just maybe, you can convince strangers to live with each other.' Airbnb subsequently won a spot on their three-month start-up programme – and the rest is history.

STRATEGY VS TACTICS

Marco (not his real name), a coaching client, had been the interim head of his division for the past twelve months, after his line manager fell seriously ill and decided to take early retirement. In line with the organisation's policy, after a year, Marco had to reapply for the role and compete with internal and external candidates.

In his initial interview, although he had incredible experience and had been doing a brilliant job, the panel questioned whether he was strategic enough in the role. This completely threw him. What did they mean? Were they right? Maybe they *were* right. After all, he had just done his job for decades; what did he know about being strategic?

We worked through what being strategic and strategic thinking really mean in practice and fitted this to a whole host of Marco's own amazing experiences. He smashed the final interview – and is now enjoying his role without the word 'interim'. He has also realised what's required to be more strategic vs more tactical – and how to manage the balance of the two.

Why strategy matters

At the heart of every successful business is a good strategy.

P&G focuses on building and growing a portfolio of trusted market-leading brands by emphasising product innovation, operational efficiency and a deep understanding of consumer needs.

Netflix focuses on leading the global streaming market by investing heavily in original content, data-driven personalisation and international expansion.

LEGO® focuses on inspiring creativity and learning through high-quality, engaging play experiences while expanding into digital entertainment, education and global markets.

However, good strategy is surprisingly uncommon. I've worked with hundreds of organisations and thousands of teams within those organisations, and not many had a clear collective understanding of their strategy (certainly not when I first met them, of course…). Many had a plan of sorts, though this was usually near-term and sometimes quite vague. Often, it was understood by just a small group of people or, in a few cases, only the group leader.

Nearly all these teams came to recognise the need for a clear shared strategy and sense of direction, as well as a well-defined plan of action. The majority also recognised the need for a vision or ambition – and how helpful it would be to get collectively clear on what's in vs out of scope over the coming years.

Most recognised the immense benefits that a strategy would provide not only to their colleagues, but also their customers, partners and other stakeholders. The primary reasons are:

- It would help to align people, improving the sharing of knowledge and understanding.

- It would help define and prioritise the most pressing challenges.

- It would create more autonomy – subsequently helping to drive innovation and incremental progress.

- It would provide clarity and energy, encouraging decisiveness and action.

- It would create confidence. Those lofty ambitions start to feel achievable.

A clear strategy helps to focus people on what matters most – and what doesn't matter at all. I should add that many teams and organisations do OK without ever having a clearly defined and communicated strategy. As I dig deeper, though, and work alongside these teams, I often discover one or both of two things. They do have a strategy – but it's in the minds of the most senior leaders (especially true of founders), and / or if that strategy is established and communicated, performance metrics improve dramatically.

The strategist

Strategy is about people. Developing good strategy is therefore dependent on the skills and attributes of the people involved.

For example, good strategists will look to harness the power of diversity. They will include new, different people in the strategy creation process. They will seek alternative perspectives from many possibly contradictory sources. They will look at problems and opportunities from an outside-in perspective. They will embrace complexity, hold tensions and balance paradoxes. They will focus on what they might be able to influence indirectly as much as on what they can directly control. They will make space to think – critically and creatively. They will look ahead, anticipating the moves of others. They will be willing to make bold decisions quickly, ensuring action is taken, lessons are learned and progress is made.

'Strategist' is not a term we hear in our day-to-day lives. It is more of a 'business thing'. Being strategic is a set of skills, behaviours, practices and principles, but it's not something that is widely taught or encouraged in formal business education, certainly not outside leadership development.

However, somewhat ironically, many of the disqualifiers for being a good strategist are consistently taught, encouraged and often embedded into organisational cultures and behaviours. They are seen, for example, in the way hierarchies exist, how decisions are made and even in how the majority of meetings are run.

With this in mind, I started to ask myself how the best strategists I have met in my career became like that. Was it chance? Was it luck?

There is, of course, a degree of talent, genetics, fortune and circumstance in everyone's story, but the people in this particular population have all worked hard to become who they are today – and continue to improve and develop. As I reflected on this many years ago, I saw patterns and similarities, and observed the same traits, characteristics and attributes again and again.

These attributes – based on first-hand experience and ongoing research – are essential to being a world-class strategist. They range from the inwardly focused (knowing who you want to be) to the externally focused (the impact you want to have), and form the core of the strategic mastery framework that underpins this book.

That is coming up shortly. First, let me introduce you to Billie.

Enter Billie

Being world class at all the traits I identified is not something I've ever seen in any one person – unless they are a Jedi Knight – so let me paint a somewhat imaginary picture.

Meet Billie. We all know a Billie, either as an individual or as an amalgam of people. We like Billie, we want to be Billie.

Malcolm Gladwell's book *Blink* talks about the elusive 'it'.[8] We know that Billie has got it because we see it in action, but we can't quite define it. The chapters throughout the book will give you a breakdown of the traits that we see Billie using each day, but here's a taster.

Billie starts the day absorbing the world's news from multiple different sources, ever-**curious and open to learning**. On her commute, she takes in what she sees and hears around her. No phone in her hand, no earphones on her head. She smiles at people she encounters.

At the office, the serious work begins, as she catches up with the team in the kitchen, getting the gossip and the latest on recent developments. Billie gathers ideas and opinions, facts and examples from people like a boy scout collects badges. She is an **active listener**, generous and supportive, but knows when to challenge as she is a **critical thinker**. Everyone loves to talk to Billie and she loves to talk to everyone.

Billie is **future-focused**. Her morning is spent working on the future vision and strategy of the business. The assembled team comprises of half her own leadership team and a selection of people representing other areas of the business and wider ecosystem, including some she has limited working knowledge of. This is because Billie is **collaborative and inclusive**, and also **comfortable with uncertainty**.

Everyone is sharing their opinions and ideas honestly and openly, actively seeking feedback and challenge. Billie pays close attention to what isn't being said, as much as to what is, conscious of both the dynamics in the team and the potential blindspots and underlying assumptions. This enables her to remain **persuasive and influential**.

At lunchtime, a crisis occurs – typically as Billie is halfway through her favourite sandwich. She calmly gathers the facts and works out what's gone wrong, being cautious about what her team is assuming, while listening carefully to a handful of selected opinions. Billie clearly frames the issue, **decisive and action focused**, setting out and weighing up her options, categorising the decision. Then she acts – clearing time in her diary for tomorrow to ensure she can reflect on and learn from any potential consequences of her actions.

Between finishing work and returning home, Billie reflects on the day's events. She knows that this daily practice helps her to continually become more **self-aware**, more conscious of her own thoughts, beliefs and emotions – and how these influence her decisions, mindset and behaviours.

That night, if time permits, Billie reads another chapter of her favourite detective novel, just to keep her creative juices flowing. It is important to her to be **creative and imaginative**.

We will unpack the traits we see Billie using over the course of the book. First, let's explore how I have tied them together into a simple, teachable framework of twelve practices.

The strategic mastery framework

This framework sets out the twelve key practices of a world-class strategist. Get good at all of these and you'll not only be a damn fine strategist, you'll probably qualify as a Jedi Knight to rival Yoda. As the saying goes, 'Teach a man to fish…'

There are four levels to the framework. Each of these levels introduces a set of practices, with the lower levels underpinning those higher up. Developmentally, there is a natural progression, so the more you improve your Level 1 skills, the better you will be at Levels 2, 3 and 4.

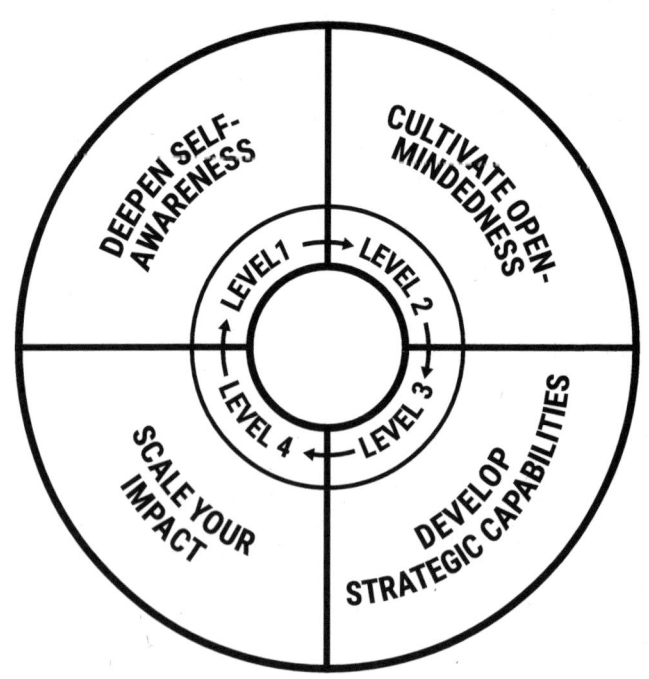

Importantly, these practices are not mutually exclusive, but this framework is not to be seen as analogous to a house of cards. If you happen to dive into the chapter on acting decisively, for example, you might start to see why you will benefit from coming back to the earlier chapters on deepening self-awareness, listening or thinking critically. This is what I refer to as vertical development.

In fact, deepening self-awareness is the foundational level (Level 1), as it is to all sustainable self-development. Being more self-aware and intentionally becoming conscious of oneself forms the bedrock supporting all great leaders and strategists.

Levels 2 to 4 each contain three behaviours, with each level becoming increasingly complex and requiring more practice and experience. Together, they equate to an ability to have far greater impact, effectively and at scale, personally and professionally. Each of these levels also spans how you might develop inwardly and outwardly, from being more inwardly or internally focused (ie who you want to be) to being more outwardly or externally focused (ie the impact you want to have).

The Level 2 practices are focused on cultivating your open-mindedness – being curious to learn; being present and listening actively; being rational, objective and critical in your thinking and your evaluation. With those building blocks in place, Level 3 explores developing your strategic capabilities – unlocking creativity, managing uncertainty and being future-focused or future-orientated.

With the first three levels mastered, you need to develop your Level 4 practices to have a genuine lasting impact on the world around you. These practices are acting decisively, collaborating inclusively and influencing effortlessly.

Being strategic isn't a secretive dark art and it shouldn't be perceived as such. It is achievable if you follow the strategic mastery framework.

INNER DEVELOPMENT GOALS

As a strategist, I've found that much of my client work over the last few decades has naturally incorporated the United Nation's (UN's) Sustainable Development Goals (SDGs) – against which progress has been depressingly slow. At the same time, as a leadership coach, I've seen much of my client work align to the UN's Inner Development Goals (IDGs), which work towards accelerating the SDGs and a more sustainable future.[9]

The IDGs provide a brilliant framework against which to develop leadership effectiveness – individually, as teams and as organisations – providing five key areas of focus on twenty-three skillsets. It was only as I approached the publication date of this book that I realised the crossover between the two. Maybe being strategic is more important than I first realised!

Let me come back to Roger Martin. In a *Harvard Business Review* article, he talks about how strategy meetings often descend into 'adversarial position-taking'.[10] As someone who has designed and facilitated thousands of strategy meetings, I completely agree.

Fortunately for many of us in the business world, Roger Martin encourages people to remove this common blocker by asking what he describes as 'the most important question in strategy':

What would have to be true?

In one of his own first-hand experiences of adversarial position-taking, Martin decided to shift the dialogue from everyone discussing what they thought was true to what they believed would have to be true for the option on the table to be the right choice. 'It was magic,' he states. 'Clashing views turned into collaboration on really understanding the logic of the options.'

In my own strategy-related work, and in many other types of creative, innovative or coaching-related endeavours, I encourage people not just to take something at face value, but to be curious. I encourage them to think differently, think laterally, think sideways.

In your next strategy meeting, consider asking questions such as:

- 'What else could it be?'

- 'What if it wasn't that?'

- 'What would happen if…?'

Alternatively, stick with Roger Martin's question – especially if people are starting to dig their heels in about what is true. Ask, 'What would have to be true?'

Here's a simple example: the leaders of a coffee store franchise are considering expanding into a new country where it doesn't currently operate. The typical question might be, 'Will opening stores there be successful?', but that's a closed question, and hard to answer without making many assumptions.

Instead, try asking, 'What would have to be true for expanding into this country to succeed?' Now they will generate a list of assumptions that they can proactively test. Instead of debating opinions, they will evaluate specific, testable conditions.

Strategy is ultimately about people – their choices, decisions, priorities, aligning effort and focus. In many workshops I run, especially near the end of an in-depth strategic leadership or strategic thinking-focused programme, people often reflect on how it's changed – and challenged – the way they think. In a good way.

It has made them realise that much of the time, they have never really paid attention to the way they thought (their metacognition) or how they might improve their thinking skills and abilities. They certainly hadn't thought that much about how others think – and how better understanding this might benefit everyone!

In fact, even though they usually arrive wearing a professional hat, they are often surprised by how much strategy is about human behaviour – including the way we think, act and feel. If strategy is about people – guess what? So is life!

Actions

- **Reflect**: Write down how you currently define strategy vs planning and / or being strategic vs being tactical. Identify specific examples from your own work and life. Compare and contrast your reflections.

- **Experiment**: Work through Roger Martin's strategy choice cascade using a subject that you're familiar with, either from your business or personal life. Define your winning aspiration, identifying where to play and how to win.

- **Audit**: Identify where in your work or life you are potentially planning and executing without strategy. Reflect and adjust accordingly.

- **Explain**: Describe your strategy to someone in a few short sentences, before inviting thoughts, feedback and questions (the more, the better). Is your strategy as clear and congruent as it could be?

- **Study Billie**: Think about the skills and characteristics that Billie demonstrates. Who do you know personally that embodies some of these skills and traits? What might you learn from your observations and reflections? How might you embody some of these traits yourself?

Key takeaways

- Being strategic is a superpower. This is true in life as much as in work. It requires a mindset shift, not just tools, and it's learnable.

- Strategy is different to planning. Strategy involves choice, direction and long-term positioning. It connects intentions to outcomes through meaningful choice. Clear strategy boosts alignment, autonomy and performance.

- Having a plan will most likely lessen anxiety. Being strategic – making tough choices – may do the opposite, certainly initially, but this is your growth and development opportunity.

- Most of the world's high-performing organisations have a clear strategy. Surprisingly, having a good, robust, well-understood strategy in business is uncommon.

- This book provides a powerful development framework to help you become a competent, capable strategist. It comprises four levels, and though there is a natural progression, you can access this framework from any point.

Remember Billie? Billie knows the difference between a plan and a strategy, and that strategy must come first. She embodies all the traits of a great strategist, and as we will see, she embraces the twelve practices of the strategic mastery framework. Billie's world is a happy, successful and enviable place to be, but this isn't down to luck. This is down to Billie's hard work to develop herself and those around her.

We can all learn to be more like Billie.

www.teammandarin.com/ resources/bemorestrategic

2
The Foundation Practices

S elf-awareness is of prime importance in becoming a great strategist and competent strategic thinker. I have seen first-hand how raising self-awareness helps to unlock people's ability to think more clearly, critically, creatively; to solve problems and identify opportunities; to make better, bolder decisions in work and in life. As you explore aspects of how you learn these skills, you realise that so much of what limits your potential today hinges around your beliefs, thoughts, feelings and behaviours – all of which can be better understood and potentially changed.

How do you raise your own self-awareness? By understanding what really makes you tick!

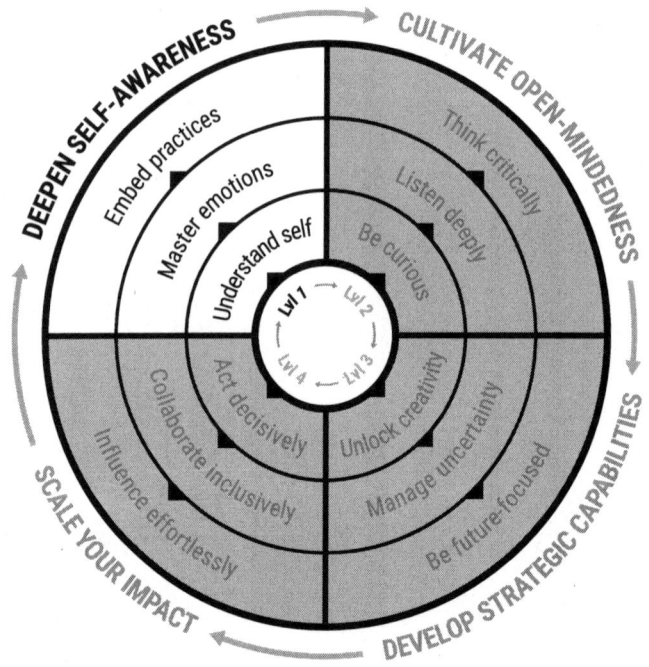

How to raise self-awareness is often explored in leadership development programmes, especially in large organisations. It is sometimes referred to as becoming a more conscious leader. Leaders are, of course, everywhere – in schools, theatres, sports teams, charities, social groups, even families – but many do not have access to this type of development.

In the introduction, I referred to the need for vertical development. Although you could approach developing strategic thinking and awareness horizontally by building your competency, which would be extremely helpful, it is only part of the picture. To truly develop in this area, you also need to understand the mindsets that underpin and influence how you think, feel and act, and develop your ability to perceive and make meaning at more complex levels.

To be a great strategist, able to develop a robust strategy – for life as much as for work – that you genuinely believe in and commit to executing, you have to build capacity and capability. Self-awareness, a trait and practice demonstrated by leaders as diverse as Marcus Aurelius to the Dalai Lama, is key to vertical development.

Here's a simple analogy. Many people set themselves New Year's resolutions – and quite a few involve getting fitter or losing weight, so they join a gym, buy the latest trainers, download fitness apps etc. This helps – but those who understand why they want these changes, and face up to the underlying beliefs that might get in the way, are far more likely to achieve a sustained shift or change.

What does self-awareness mean in practice? How do you do it, why is it so important, and how does it help you to be a more confident strategist – and a more impactful and influential leader?

Being more self-aware means better understanding your own values, beliefs and behaviours. It's about recognising your blindspots, assumptions and preconceptions – including what might be holding you back. It's about exploring the judgements you might be making – albeit subconsciously – about yourself and others. It's about being aware of how present you are to people, how well you listen and what you choose to hear, say or ask. It's how and why you make certain decisions and influence others – directly or indirectly.

It's also about understanding your strengths, realised and unrealised, and your weaknesses, learned behaviours and… well, just stuff you are not good at. It's about knowing how to use those strengths wisely, and improve and develop accordingly.

This understanding enables you to self-manage and self-regulate better.

A client recently told me that through raising their self-awareness, they have made fundamental shifts in their mindset, beliefs and behaviours from which there is no going back. They described how they now see everything more clearly, from a higher, better level and perspective, professionally and personally. They have let go of their less helpful beliefs and behaviours – and consequently been able to let in new beliefs and behaviours.

In metaphorical terms, they have turned into a butterfly. They can never go back to being a caterpillar.

This shift in mindset and behaviour makes the work in Levels 2–4 possible. It isn't necessarily about transformation or a life reset, but about continuous growth that can begin at any time.

To become more self-aware, it helps to understand how the human brain works – and also how it develops. After all, your self is hosted in your brain.

How the brain works

Personally, having a good knowledge of how my own thoughts, feelings and behaviours interconnect has been incredibly useful, and I continue to better understand that. As my career has progressed to coach, facilitator and often someone else's hired thinker, my interest in neuroscience, psychology and physiology has deepened. After all, I spend each and every day immersed in groups of people. Plus my late father was a clinical psychiatrist, and my wife is a qualified psychologist, so there really is no escape!

Let's first do some myth-busting. People often talk about being left or right brained – myself included, even though I would suggest that being a good strategist is a whole brain activity.

What's fact vs fiction?

The human brain is made up of two halves or hemispheres that each control the opposite side of the body. As brilliantly explained in the fantastic *Kay's Anatomy*, that means that 'your right brain looks after your left nostril and your left elbow; and your left brain looks after your right ankle and your right butt cheek'.[11] My children remember this fact more than most others.

In addition to coordinating your left side, your right hemisphere is responsible for the big picture: putting things into context, reading between the lines, recognising body language and so on. The left side is more focused on detail. It provides clarity and mechanically uses tools and words that we already know.

The two halves of the brain give us two different pictures of the world that we combine into one, but one half tends to be dominant. Are you left or right brain dominant?

Here's a simple way to find out:

- Fold your hands, interlocking your fingers. Which thumb is on top? Note down A for right thumb, B for left thumb.

- Draw a straight line on the ground and walk along it with your eyes closed. Then open your eyes. In which direction have you diverted from the line? A is to the right, B to the left.

- Look at your desktop – what state is it in? A for tidy and organised, B for chaotic.

- Draw a Q on your forehead with your finger (don't use a pen). How did you do it? A so that a viewer can read it on your forehead, B so that you could read it.

- Look at the objects in front of you. Now close one eye. Which one did you close? A is left eye, B right eye.

More A's indicates left dominance, more B's indicates right dominance.

Left brain dominance is associated with logical thinking, analysis and language skills. These people might prefer to learn through structured methodical approaches – and approach problems through analysis, planning and critical reasoning.

Right brain dominance is associated with creativity, intuition and spatial reasoning. These people might prefer to learn with visual aids, storytelling and hands-on activities – and approach problems using imagination, gut feel and a more holistic view.

Understanding your own and other people's approach can help you balance your methods and collaborate more effectively with them by complementing different strengths. However, knowing your dominance is a starting point, not a limitation.

The image below highlights a few key areas of the brain, those that are more relevant to the chapters of this book.

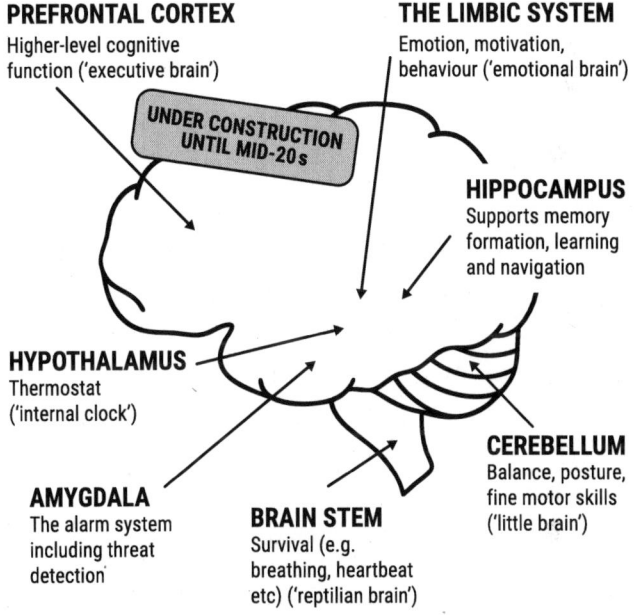

PREFRONTAL CORTEX
Higher-level cognitive function ('executive brain')

UNDER CONSTRUCTION UNTIL MID-20s

THE LIMBIC SYSTEM
Emotion, motivation, behaviour ('emotional brain')

HIPPOCAMPUS
Supports memory formation, learning and navigation

HYPOTHALAMUS
Thermostat ('internal clock')

CEREBELLUM
Balance, posture, fine motor skills ('little brain')

AMYGDALA
The alarm system including threat detection

BRAIN STEM
Survival (e.g. breathing, heartbeat etc) ('reptilian brain')

Key areas of the brain

- **Prefrontal cortex** – responsible for high-level cognitive function such as problem solving, planning and decision making; often referred to as the 'executive brain'. Is part of the cerebral cortex, the grey matter (neuron cell bodies) that covers the entire surface of the brain's two hemispheres and constitutes ~40% of the brain's weight.

- **Cerebellum** – in the brain's two hemispheres that coordinate movements on corresponding sides of the body, regulating posture and balance. Also plays a less well-understood role in emotional regulation, language processing and social cognition. Often referred to as the 'little brain'.

- **Brainstem** – connects the cerebellum with the spinal cord (actually connects everything!), and relays messages between the brain and the rest of the body via nerve pathways. Often referred to as the 'reptilian brain' and is responsible for basic life functions (eg heartbeat, breathing, survival instincts).

- **Hypothalamus** – centrally located and connected to multiple brain systems; maintains homeostasis by regulating body temperature; also regulates circadian rhythms (the brain's 'internal clock') and monitors blood chemistry triggering hunger and thirst. Influences emotion by interacting with the limbic system (see below) especially in generating physical responses (eg heart rate when fearful).

- **Hippocampus** – plays a central role in forming long-term memories, learning new information, and spatial memory and navigation (eg mental maps of environments). Interestingly, it is the shape of a seahorse, which is what 'hippocampus' means in Greek!

- **Limbic system** – a network of structures deep within the brain involved in emotion, motivation, behaviour and memory; integrates emotional experiences with bodily responses, helping to drive survival behaviours such as fear, pleasure and aggression. Includes some of the components described above, including the hippocampus and hypothalamus – and also contains the amygdala, which I'll explain separately given its relevance to this section of this book.

- **Amygdala** – part of the limbic system, acting as the brain's alarm system. Located under each hemisphere (yes, there are two!), it is directly involved in emotional reactivity, so calming or retraining amygdala responses (eg through mindfulness, CBT) is especially relevant to the **mastering emotions** practice of Level 1. The amygdala interacts with the hypothalamus to trigger the fight or flight response to threat (activating the sympathetic nervous system) and also has connections with the reward system, especially in emotional learning and motivation.

Learning about the amygdala hijack was a personal game changer. Originating from Daniel Goleman's work on emotional intelligence,[12] the term describes how emotions can swamp the brain and overwhelm a person with feelings and thoughts, making it incredibly hard to think straight or behave rationally.

Learning why this happens – and the role the amygdala is playing when it goes into overdrive and makes us obsess about whatever is causing our distress or upset – is a useful step on the self-awareness journey.

Understand self – the human iceberg

At the start of this chapter, I said that to raise your self-awareness, you need to better understand what makes you tick; what *really* matters to you. What are your needs and concerns? What are your values and beliefs? What motivates you? What excites you? What are you afraid of? What drives your decisions and underpins your behaviours, especially when you're tired, hungry or under stress? How can you **master your emotions**?

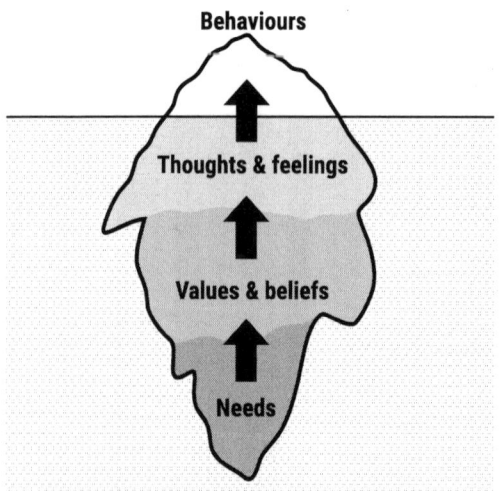

The human iceberg: Adapted from Edward T Hall's cultural iceberg model[13]

A useful way to envisage this is by thinking about a human as an iceberg. This is an idea with multiple origins, including neurologist Sigmund Freud, who developed a 'topographical model of the mind'[14] to describe the conscious and unconscious mind with the visible tip being the former (thoughts we're aware of) and the submerged portion being the latter (hidden desires, fears and drives).

Let's work from the top. The first step in raising our self-awareness is to recognise that everyone else only sees about 10% of us – what we do and say. To put it another way, others are judging us predominantly on what we do and say, which is just 10% of what makes us, us.

The other 90% resides below the surface. People's awareness and understanding of this 90% vary considerably, and yet it is this which influences our behaviour and what others actually see. I still find this incredible, when I stop and think about what it means in practice.

Raising our self-awareness and developing vertically helps us to lower the metaphorical water level and understand more of our iceberg. This is why the first task of a developing leader – or strategist – is to become more self-aware.

We will now work our way down the iceberg, exploring and understanding more about:

- Our behaviours, ie what we do and say

- Our thoughts and feelings (emotions)

- Our values and beliefs (limiting or otherwise)

- Our needs (met and unmet, ie right down at the bottom, driving everything above them – our life story)

All of these will regularly be referred to throughout later chapters. Looking back at the strategy mastery framework, we can clearly see the role this model plays in, for example, how well we're able to listen deeply, think critically, be future-focused, manage uncertainty and act decisively.

Behaviours

Think about the last challenging conversation you were involved in. How aligned were what you actually said (ie the words you used, your tone of voice, etc) and how you appeared (ie facial expressions, gestures etc) with what you really thought and felt?

What about the other person? What could you not see or hear? What assumptions were you making?

Perhaps something unexpected happened in the conversation. It didn't go as you hoped. Perhaps you said or did something that angered or upset the other person. Maybe you were unhelpfully triggered and responded in a way that you now regret, but you couldn't explain why that happened or, in the moment, control your behaviour.

This is why we need to develop vertically (work a little further down the iceberg) if we really want to master our emotions and change behaviours sustainably.

Thoughts

Thoughts are the voices in our heads – our self-talk. Everyone has a version of this. We'll explore more about our thinking processes in Chapter 5 on critical thinking.

To become more self-aware, more tuned into your thought processes (and feelings and emotions, as we'll explore shortly), you may want to experiment with popular practices such as mindfulness and meditation. These practices help you focus on the present moment and develop a deeper understanding of your thoughts and feelings without judgement.

Personally, I have learned to recognise where certain anxieties manifest in my body. This might be sudden (an alarm going off in my mind, but showing up in my gut or lower back), or over time, where I feel it more across my shoulders (and it shows in my posture).

Simple breathing techniques such as box breathing[15] and, if time permits, meditation techniques such as Dynamic Mind Practice allow me to deliberately turn my attention inwards and ground myself (and shift out of higher frequency beta brain waves). This removes the sense of threat from the body, which in turn lets the brain know that there is no threat and I'm able to proceed. Interestingly, these same techniques enable us to engage areas of the brain that are responsible for higher-level cognitive function and rational thinking.

Feelings

We ask about each other's feelings every day – but what is a feeling?

Feelings are emotions that rise up in us.

In Chapter 4: 'Be (More) Present, Be A Listener', we explore how to manage your emotions in difficult situations. However, it's here at the deepen self-awareness level where you need to start learning how to master your feelings and emotions at any time.

I often start group coaching sessions with a routine check-in, which includes asking people how they feel. The majority of people – and I'm talking thousands – do not respond with a description of how they feel. Instead, they tend to describe what they are thinking, or what they have been doing recently – and usually tell everyone how busy they are. Interestingly, depending on the context, I might ask the question again – and this time, far more people move down their icebergs and articulate their feelings and emotions.

Why do so many smart, well-educated individuals struggle to state how they are feeling? In a world where leaders embrace concepts such as emotional intelligence, empathetic leadership and psychological safety, it seems that many people have lost – or possibly never had – a vital connection with understanding or articulating what their own bodies are telling them. Maybe they're just too busy to be paying attention.

Is articulating our true feelings actually a far more important skillset than we realise? The answer is an emphatic yes. Without mastering our feelings, we cannot master Level 1 of the strategic mastery framework, the foundation on which the rest of the levels are built.

Try this:

- Take a moment now to press pause.

- If you are able, sit upright with your feet on the floor, hands on your lap.

- Lower your gaze and take three slow, deep breaths.

- Notice not only what you're thinking, but how you're feeling.

- How might you describe those feelings? How do they relate to your thoughts and behaviours?

A tool called an emotions wheel (or feelings wheel), widely used in coaching and therapy, helps to accurately identify and label the different feelings and emotions, which are often more complex and varied than we first imagine. They may fluctuate rapidly; some may say that they feel a combination of emotions all at once. Being able to clearly describe how you feel – and how you have felt historically – is extremely good for your wellbeing, let alone how useful it is in managing and leading yourself and others.

Values and beliefs

To find these, we travel a level deeper in the human iceberg.

Our values are what we hold as being most important to us in life. What we value is driven by our life experiences.

Our beliefs are the opinions, principles and doctrines that we, as individuals, hold as being true (unconsciously, for most people). These beliefs – our stories – become our filter on the world (however distorted).

We make hundreds, if not thousands of decisions every day, individually and collectively. Every decision that we make is a reflection of our values and our beliefs. Ideally, these are always directed towards a specific purpose – but for many people, this purpose is lost or lacking.

Needs

Our perception of whether or not our needs have been met drives our values and our beliefs, and our values and beliefs drive everything else – our thoughts, feelings and, ultimately, our behaviours.

Abraham Maslow first published his Hierarchy of Needs in 1943.[16] It remains just as relevant today.

An overview of Maslow's hierarchy of needs

Level	Explanation
1. Physiological	Meeting basic physiological needs.
2. Safety	Protection from physical and psychological threats, fear and anxiety. The need for order, structure and security.

3 Love and belonging	Acceptance, membership, affection, belonging, feeling loved and wanted.
4. Self-esteem	Respect and liking yourself and others. Strength, competence, status, achievement and freedom.
5. Self-actualisation	To do what you must to become fully yourself. To develop your own individuality. To become everything you are capable of becoming.

How our needs need to be met is analogous to a house of cards. We must start at the bottom and work up, meeting tiers of needs in order. Only once our physiological and psychological (safety in the diagram) needs are met can we grow and self-actualise, becoming everything that we can become.

As we'll explore in Chapter 3: 'Be (More) Curious, Be A Learner', it is our fears that hold us back – our fears that our needs won't be met. (See the 'Out of the comfort zone' section in Chapter 3.)

Master emotions – mindset, beliefs and triggers

It can be useful to understand how our beliefs and mindsets are formed.

When we are very young, as our brain grows and develops, our amygdala forms to keep us safe. Neither our rational brain nor our language is fully developed at this point, and so we only experience events through our emotions, as pain or pleasure.

These memories get laid down in the emotional part of the brain, ie as feelings, because at that point, we have no language for them. They then form our beliefs and mindsets. There are two particularly useful insights to take from this short neuroscience lesson.

Beliefs

First, whichever needs are deficient in our formative years will distort our perceptions. The greater the deficiency of these needs, the more we distort reality to fit our expectations and treat others according to their usefulness in helping us satisfy our needs. This becomes our filter on the world.

Our beliefs will have helped us as accelerators – we are here, safe and successful – but they may have acted or are currently acting as a hindrance – our brakes. The good news is we as humans now understand neuroplasticity – the ability of the brain to rewire itself. With the right support and practices, and where it's useful to do so, we can change our beliefs.

How does this help us to be more strategic in the way we think and act? Our beliefs influence how we see the world – our biases, assumptions and preconceptions, how we see patterns, possibilities, risks and so on. If you look back at the strategic mastery framework in Chapter 1, you will find it hard to see where beliefs aren't relevant.

The second insight is this: as we get older, we continually scan to check that we're safe. When we see a potential threat, our brain looks for where we've seen that threat before. If that happens to be when we were very young and didn't have the language to describe it, our reaction naturally comes out as an emotional response. Hence why, as mature adults, we make triggered responses that can seem out of proportion.

How does knowing this help us to be more strategic in the way we think and act? We can learn to control and regulate our emotions, communicate effectively, build relationships, influence others and make decisions.

EXERCISE – Spotting your defaults

At the end of the day, ask yourself:

- What strong emotions did I feel today?
- What triggered them?
- What belief or fear might sit underneath?
- How did I respond – and how 'strategic' or useful was that?
- What could I try next time?

This is good pattern recognition – spotting your own defaults, so that you can shift them. The more you do this, the more agency you build.

Before we move on to look at triggers, it's important to recognise the fundamental difference between being passive and being composed. Being passive is a reactive mindset – pulling back or deferring, reflecting a belief that the power lies elsewhere. Being composed is a creative mindset – holding steady under pressure, creating space for clarity to emerge.

Triggers

How would you react if a bear jumped out at you? Most likely, one of three snap responses:

- Fight – take it on, challenge it, lean in
- Flight – the opposite, run away
- Freeze – you don't know what to do

These snap responses are where the brain hijacks our behaviour, especially in times of high stress. In a work situation, when the pressure's on, people often snap, hijacked by a stress response. For example, a particularly controlling or forceful colleague might make you tense. You then start defending your ideas rather than exploring them openly. The nervous system registers a threat and the fight response kicks in.

There are two lesser-known responses: fawn, meaning you try to please the bear, and flop, when you become apathetic and cease to care. Neither is recommended!

Why do I ask that? When you are triggered, it is broadly related to one of three fundamental human needs:

- To be safe

- To be loved

- To be good enough (self-worth)

When you are triggered, being self-aware becomes crucial. You then recognise in the moment that it's about you and not about anyone else. This allows you to take ownership.

A brief period, six to ten seconds (depending on who you ask), of breathing calmly will allow your amygdala to relax. Normal service can then resume, and you will be able to see more clearly the choices available to you.

PAUSE FOR THOUGHT

Annie (not her real name), a coaching client, knew that she had a tendency to respond less than helpfully to people in the moment. If someone disagreed with her or challenged her on certain topics, she would flare up – and this was starting to impact not only her career, but also her relationships.

Through practice and hard work, Annie is now able to 'slow down time' – creating a required pause in conversations that may previously have triggered her. Rather than snap back, she notices her immediate feelings and judgements and where these potentially originate, then deliberately shifts to a position of curiosity (creative mindset). She will perhaps say, completely genuinely, 'That's interesting.'

> This version of vertical development has become natural and in the moment for Annie, and her relationships at work and home have improved dramatically, as has her wellbeing.

Mindset

Your mindset relates to your beliefs about your talent and abilities, and in simple terms creates your mental model. This shapes your capacity to learn and develop, to create, to lead – amongst other things – and has implications for your education, relationships, how you parent a child etc.

Psychologist Dr Carol Dweck of Stanford University first introduced the concept of growth mindset in her 2007 book *Mindset*.[17] In her famous study, schoolchildren were presented with a selection of puzzles ranging in difficulty. Some opted for the easier ones; others chose the more challenging ones. The first group were scared to get it wrong/lacked belief. The latter group recognised an opportunity to learn and grow. Unconcerned about being right or wrong, they had a growth mindset.

Take a moment to consider how conscious and unconscious thoughts affect what you want and whether you will succeed in attaining it. Dweck suggests that altering even the simplest of these thoughts or beliefs can impact nearly every aspect of your life.

We'll return to the importance of mindset in Chapter 3: 'Be (More) Curious, Be A Learner'.

Embed practices

Developing habits and practices to build self-awareness enables our brains to save energy by operating on auto-pilot. Here are some of the most helpful and relevant habits and practices you can try.

Reflection (eg journaling). Write down your thoughts, emotions and experiences daily or weekly. Keep the human iceberg in mind. Reflect on situations that went well and those that didn't, noting your reactions and what influenced them. Don't forget to celebrate your achievements.

Personally, I journal through the lens of my values and beliefs – continuously checking in on my intentions, habits and practices. This ensures that I remain true to myself and my purpose.

Ask yourself questions such as, 'What did I learn about myself today?' and 'How did I react to challenges?' Learn to identify and label your emotions accurately using the emotions wheel described earlier. Pay attention to your triggers and patterns, reflecting on recurring behaviours or thoughts which can reveal underlying beliefs or tendencies.

Experiment with different meditation and/or mindfulness practices, as discussed in the human iceberg section. There are apps available to support these practices, many of which are free to use.

Seek out feedback from people you trust. Be open and receptive to this feedback, focusing on understanding rather than defending or justifying.

Ask people to share their feedback on your strengths and potential areas for growth. Simple approaches include 'What works well and even better if?' or the 3-2-1 method, which is 3x things you're doing well, 2x areas to improve, 1x thing to stop doing. In professional settings, use well-structured feedback tools to gather accurate, honest and constructive insights (eg 360 feedback).

Understand your values and beliefs. Repeat the statement: 'I believe this because...' then challenge your assumptions – 'Why do I believe this? How is it serving me today and in the future?'

Practise empathy and perspective-taking. For example, put yourself in others' shoes and regularly ask, 'How might others perceive this situation or my actions?' Experiment with new perspectives. Try new roles, tasks or environments to challenge your existing perceptions and gain fresh insights. Engage with people who have different viewpoints or come from different backgrounds.

Practise self-compassion. Acknowledge that growth takes time and celebrate small wins.

Focus on your energy. Everything we do, from work meetings to spending time with loved ones, relies on our energy, yet many of us overlook the significance of conserving and replenishing it. It's something we often take for granted or don't think about at all. Some of the best leaders I work with operate at 90–100% only about 60–70% of the time. They have learned to iron out their energy curves with fewer peaks and troughs throughout their days.

Actions

- **Reflect**: Have a go at describing your own iceberg, identifying, labelling and tracking your surface behaviours vs deeper values and beliefs. Solicit feedback from others where useful / appropriate (eg on how you acted, behaved etc).

- **Articulate**: Use the emotions wheel (and other available resources) to improve your ability to articulate how you really feel about particular events or circumstances. It may help to journal these feelings over a period of time, eg a few minutes each and every day.

- **Mindfulness**: Experiment with various mindfulness, meditation and / or breathing techniques.

- **Feedback**: Building on or alongside 'reflect', ask two people you trust, from different areas of your life, for their thoughts on what you're doing well and where you could improve.

- **Triggers**: Track the situations that trigger you, being as specific as possible (eg pinpoint the people, the circumstances etc). Reflect on what core need, value or belief was potentially impacted, and why.

Key takeaways

- Improving our self-awareness is the foundation of becoming a better strategist – helping to drive listening and communication, critical thinking, decision making and leadership.

- Understanding elements of psychology, physiology and neuroscience helps us to understand why we – and others – think and act in certain ways, and how we might therefore change and develop aspects of our character and behaviour.

- Our behaviour – what others see – is only 10% of us. Ultimately, what shapes our thinking and drives our behaviours are our emotions, beliefs, values and needs – met and unmet – all of which sit below the metaphorical water line on the human iceberg.

- Though our mindset is shaped by past experiences, neuroplasticity means we can rewire how we think and behave.

- Triggers often stem from unmet core needs: feeling safe, feeling loved, feeling good enough (self-worth). We can explore and understand why we react to certain situations in certain ways (especially the less helpful ones) and with time, focus and practice, learn to change these patterns of behaviour.

Remember Billie? Her continuous journey to improve her self-awareness is key to her being more strategic – and a better leader. This includes aspects of how she thinks, acts and communicates.

www.teammandarin.com/
resources/bemorestrategic

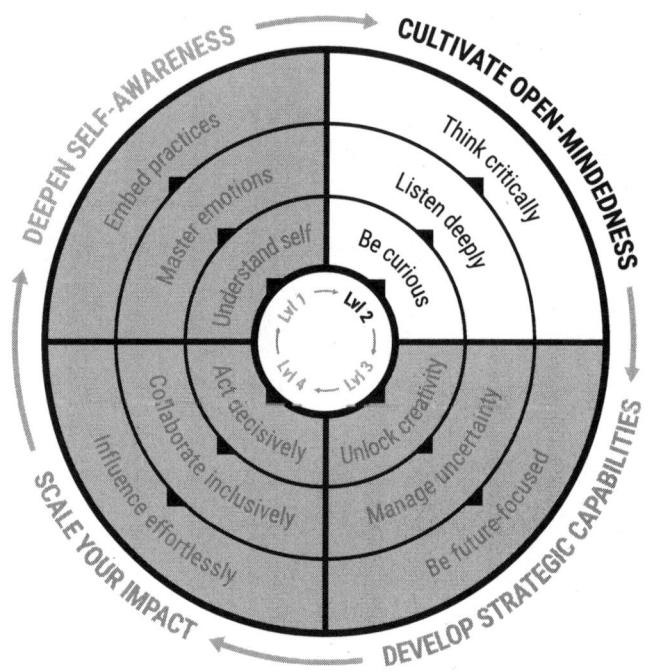

PART TWO

LEVEL 2 PRACTICES – CULTIVATE OPEN-MINDEDNESS

The skills in this section help us to be more deliberately and intentionally open-minded. This means being curious and open to learning, being present and able to listen deeply, and being critical, rational and objective in our thinking and our evaluation.

3

Be (More) Curious, Be A Learner

Strategists are truly open-minded. At the heart of being open-minded, and of great strategy, is curiosity.

Strategists are relentless question-askers. They continuously seek to identify and challenge assumptions, to make connections and discover patterns, to spot potentially unseen risks and opportunities. Being curious means having an innate desire to learn and understand, intentionally seeking to stay relevant by continually updating beliefs, frameworks and mental models.

Curiosity underpins other areas of the strategic mastery framework, so there is significant crossover between this and other chapters. For example, curiosity drives strategists to seek out different perspectives, which we will explore in more detail in Chapter 5 on critical thinking. A curious mind thrives on ambiguity and the unknown, seeing them as an opportunity to explore new possibilities and grow, a topic that we will examine in Chapter 7 on uncertainty. Learners experiment, seeking to take lessons from all their decisions and actions, successes and failures, something covered in more depth in Chapter 9 on decision making.

Great examples of people who displayed deep levels of curiosity include Albert Einstein, Marie Curie and Leonardo da Vinci.

Defining learning

The *Oxford Dictionary of English* defines learning as 'the acquisition of knowledge or skills through study, experience, or being taught'. That sounds similar to education, but there's an important difference, which is the source of much debate.

To highlight the difference, I use the well-known analogy of a young child standing in front of a hot kettle. A sign on the wall that warns the child the kettle is hot and not to touch it is education. The child touching the kettle and discovering that it is hot is learning. In military environments, you may hear the phrase, 'train for certainty, educate for uncertainty.'

In fact, though we'll explore the benefits of learning by doing in this chapter, it's important to recognise that we also learn from a moving, memorable story. What do the two have in common?

Emotions, or learning by feelings. Emotions and feelings are often far more powerful than what we do, see or hear. We'll talk more about this in Chapter 11 on influential communication.

Many people think of learning as simply absorbing information or memorising facts. This is why in many organisations, 'training' – which often involves pushing facts and information on to people – can have a bad rap. As the brilliant author Nick Shackleton-Jones points out, true learning isn't about dumping content into people's heads. This 'rote learning' lacks emotional or contextual resonance and has no significant impact on performance as a result.[18] He argues that while hands-on experience is closer to genuine learning, what really matters is combining 'learning by doing' with emotional relevance and meaningful context. In other words, not just skill training but learning that actually changes capabilities.

He also gives the example of a new person joining a team. That experience alone shakes up their behaviour as they pick up on the culture and expectations around them.

How a strategist learns

Roger Martin sets out four characteristics of a great strategic thinker. He or she 'seeks to influence what is not in [his or her] control', 'consumes information omnivorously', 'leverages abductive reasoning' and 'considers multiple variables simultaneously'.[19] The last two characteristics are explored in Chapter 5 on critical thinking; here we'll examine the first two.

Martin explains how the 'object [of strategy] is to influence behaviour of customers in the future' – even though there is no data about the future (in most cases). Music to my ears. Strategy is definitely not dragging the box up and right on your spreadsheet so that your gross revenue figure doubles. As one CEO said to his team in the middle of a workshop: 'For every business failure, I had a spreadsheet that told me it would be a great success.'

Martin also explains, '[Strategic thinkers] become skilled at thinking and deciding based on a wide variety of information that is not statistically significant and often not quantifiable either.' Strategists collect and absorb information, without bias or blinkers, from a broad range of different sources – including those beyond traditional boundaries.

This is why good strategic leaders say that an important part of their role is to 'see around corners'. In fact, I was recently catching up with an old friend, Shuja Khan, who is now the CEO of a major UK-based telecommunications and media services company. He used this exact expression when describing his responsibilities.

Remember Billie? She deliberately seeks views and opinions from outside her inner circle. We'll explore this further in other chapters, as it overlaps with our ability to think critically, think creatively and become more future-focused.

I remember working on a major consulting project many years ago – in a time when boundaries were being challenged in the more traditional industries. One of my problems was that the leadership team only looked at insight and intelligence about their own sector as defined by… their sector. They were seemingly blind to the disruption rapidly coming their way from other sectors and industries.

As we'll explore in other chapters, being strategic means being able to see the bigger picture – making connections, asking good questions, taking action and revising assumptions based on facts and events. This approach helps you to get under the skin of the real problem or issue. It means you constantly challenge yourself and others, have a growth mindset and actively seek feedback – or better still, advice – and continual improvement.

Let's explore what learning really is, how it happens and how it varies in different people. What gets in the way and what's useful to know and understand to improve your own curiosity? This will ensure you're learning as much and as fast as you possibly can, asking better questions, experimenting, being open to new ideas and embracing feedback.

How learning works

How do you prefer to learn something new? If you're similar to much of the population, it's probably along these lines:

- You watch someone else do it first.

- You then have a go at doing it yourself.

- Finally, and ideally, you teach someone else to do it.

We tend to learn by observing or by doing, which leads to better free recall of memories. The problem is, our memories are akin to a leaky bucket. Most of the information that enters our brains leaks out eventually.

Humans have both short-term and long-term memories, which helps us manage how much information we hold in our brains. The information we do store becomes the foundation for linking newly acquired knowledge with older existing knowledge. Hence why you may more than once have uttered the words, 'Ah yes, I remember this.'

To improve learning effectiveness, it's important to include both variation (eg in the modes, mediums, styles etc) and intervals (eg taking regular breaks). In his book *How We Learn*,[20] Benedict Carey discusses the spacing effect, emphasising that distributed learning – studying a little every day rather than cramming – leads to better retention. As I crammed to attain an undergraduate degree in engineering, it's a good job I've never had to build a bridge!

Carey notes, 'People learn at least as much, and retain it much longer, when they distribute – or space – their study time than when they concentrate it.' Ah, how I wish someone had told me that when I was younger! (Author makes a note to let his children know.)

As Josh Waitzkin explains in *The Art of Learning*,[21] and as we'll explore in other chapters, failure is important in the learning process. More accurately (and an important distinction), learning **from** that failure is important, not the failure itself.

Take a moment to reflect on a time when you felt that you went through a valuable learning curve. Ask yourself these questions:

- What was the situation? Who was involved?

- What did you need / have to learn? Over what timescale?

- What happened? What was the outcome or result?

- What made this situation unique compared to other situations?

Now take a moment to reflect on how that experience felt compared to other experiences. What did you notice in your responses above? What might you take forward / repeat?

How do you retain knowledge most successfully?

The Learning Pyramid, developed in the 1960s and widely attributed to the National Training Laboratories Institute in Bethel, Maine, United States, shows that teaching through participatory methods leads to far greater human recall than passive teaching methods. Although we as humans have known this for a long time, we often forget to apply it.

The pyramid shows that humans remember:

- At the lower end, just 5% of what they've learned from a lecture (eg at college), or 10% of what they learn from reading a book. Doh!

- At the higher end, approximately 75% of what they learn when they practise the learning, and 90% of what they learn when they use it immediately or to teach others. This is why we need to prioritise teaching someone else.

This is about reframing how you see learning – and having a greater openness to it. Rather than perceiving learning as being a training course that you don't have time for, see it as far more than that. Be open to learning all the time, eg by joining in a discussion, taking an opportunity to apply or teach something new, inviting and listening to feedback.

The key is then to allow time for reflection. As the saying goes, 'Slow down to speed up.'

What makes a good learner?

I often ask this question in workshops. Responses tend to include some or all of these:

- They question everything.
- They have strong motivation and self-discipline.
- They know how and when to ask for help.
- They are willing to take risks, fail and learn from their mistakes.
- They engage with the world around them.

Occasionally, someone says, 'A good learner has learning ability or a desire to learn.' This often draws comment, because it's quite a difficult concept to grasp.

Having learning ability and a desire to learn is key to being a strategist, and it's definitely something we can develop.

ROCKS AND SPONGES

Through an old school friend, who unlike the rest of us 'high flyers'(!) went on to win the Rugby World Cup, I've been lucky enough not only to watch that once-in-a-lifetime moment in the flesh (the Johnny Wilkinson drop goal) and play rugby with some of the team in a pro-am charity match (foolish), but also to hear stories about what made their high-performance environment so successful. Of the many amazing stories and insights I've gleaned over the years, it was World Cup Winning Coach Sir Clive Woodward's comments about 'talent not being enough' that always stayed with me.

Sir Clive talks about a person's teachability in terms of whether they are a rock or a sponge. I heard him speak about this a few times, and a keynote he gave at a work summit stuck with me:[22]

'If you are a sponge, you have a thirst for knowledge, you have a passion about what you do and want to learn more ... a rock on the other hand is unteachable and a bit of a know it all.'

In a successful team environment, you need a culture of learning, ie you need *all* your people to be sponges. Even just one rock is enough to vastly reduce a team's chances of winning or succeeding, which may explain some of Sir Clive's squad selections.

True high performers are sponges: they look for opportunities to learn – all the time. They don't get defensive, they crave feedback and they're willing to take considered risks.

Microsoft is one of the companies we celebrate in Chapter 9 on decision making for its genuine learning culture. This has been achieved under the guidance of the brilliant CEO, Satya Nadella – and one of his most oft repeated quotes is: 'Don't be a know-it-all. Be a learn-it-all.'[23] This encapsulates how Microsoft has embraced a collective growth mindset over the past decade.

Learning agility and the ability to unlearn

In high-performance environments, you often hear the term 'learning agility'. This means having the capacity for rapid continuous learning from experience.

As eloquently described in a *Harvard Business Review* article by Monique Valcour in 2015,[24] agile learners are good at making connections across experiences. They are able to let go of perspectives or approaches that are no longer useful. Put another way, they can unlearn things – which is an incredibly powerful and useful skill, professionally and personally.

Some people that I train, coach and mentor are, to varying degrees, struggling in their roles as leaders because they have, perhaps unwittingly, continued to manage rather than lead. They haven't recognised that they may need to unlearn some of their formerly useful managerial skills and practices. They need to let go before they can let in new leadership competences and capabilities and, importantly, beliefs.

Out of the comfort zone

How does it feel when you're comfortable performing a task or activity? It might feel natural, easy. You might feel relaxed, safe, that your needs are met (see Maslow's hierarchy in the previous chapter). You might also feel bored.

This is your comfort zone.

How does it feel when you're learning something new or trying something for the first time? It might feel exciting. You might feel unsure, unsafe or uncertain. You might feel uncomfortable.

This is your learning zone.

If your learning curve happens to be incredibly steep, too steep, how might that feel? At the extreme, maybe you'll feel outright terror. We don't want that!

Stepping out of your comfort zone triggers fear as you face the unknown and the uncertain. Once you move past fear, learning starts. Over time, as you move between the comfort and learning zones repeatedly, deliberately and proactively, that feeling of fear dissipates. Don't step out too far and make sure you come back to the comfort zone, but step out again, and repeat.

Soon growth takes root and you move up to the next level. What was once new and uncertain becomes your normal.

Becoming conscious of our unmet needs brings a powerful new awareness of what really drives our thoughts, feelings and, ultimately, our behaviours. Then, sustainable change can begin. As I know from my own coaching and development journey in recent years, we quickly start the process of letting go to let in.

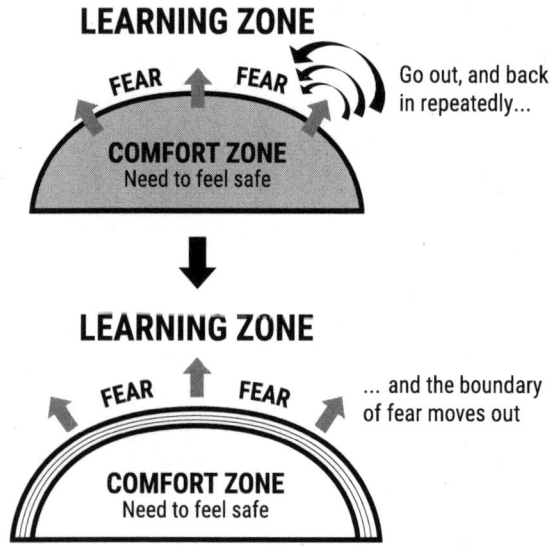

Moving beyond the comfort zone:
fear gives way to learning and growth

Here's an example. How do you feel about speaking in public?

If you find it potentially anxiety-inducing, try it, but on a small scale. Speak in a room with a few people around a table. Reflect on your experience – keep a journal or just talk through it with someone you trust.

Now find another opportunity – maybe stand at the front of a room and speak to at least ten people. Use notes, slides, stand behind a lectern. It doesn't matter. The point is that you're doing it. You are pushing those boundaries.

Keep going with this process – keep finding opportunities to push the edge of your comfort zone, always remembering to return to safety, reflect and re-energise.

However, rather than just relying on pushing the boundary out, you'll find a more effective way to learn and grow quickly is to be pulled out of your comfort zone as well. What is the most powerful source of energy to do this – the most powerful pull? A clear purpose. I know this to be true not only personally, but also through coaching others over the last ten years or so.

The author and researcher Dan Pink brilliantly explores this in his book *Drive*.[25] He says that purpose is one of the key underlying drivers of someone's intrinsic – rather than extrinsic – motivation, the others being mastery (learning something new) and autonomy (freedom to act).

Growth mindset is a learning mindset

Carol Dweck's mindset theory, introduced in the previous chapter, is highly applicable to learning. Simply being aware of the concept and understanding the connections is valuable to everyone.

Have you ever heard anyone say, 'I can't draw' or 'I'm no good at sport' or 'I could never do that'? Many people form strong beliefs that they can't and will never be able to draw or paint, or sculpt, or dance or DJ. Formed since childhood, possibly as a result of a throwaway comment by a parent or teacher, their view of the world is that there are certain people who can do those things and others who cannot. This is a mindset – informed by beliefs – but it's incorrect. We can all learn by altering our mindset about how we learn.

The main difference between a growth and a fixed mindset lies in how we view our intelligence and abilities. A fixed mindset assumes these qualities are largely unchangeable, ie we either have them or we don't (think of the examples above re drawing or dancing). A growth mindset sees intelligence and capability as flexible, with the potential to grow through effort, feedback and learning from setbacks.

This doesn't mean growth is automatic or that people always improve (though there's hope in my DJing). In fact, people with a growth mindset accept that they can regress, fail or fall short (there goes my dancing career). However, these moments are opportunities to learn and adapt.

Here's the key point I focus on in my work: mindset isn't a personality trait, it's contextual. You might have a growth mindset when learning to use new software, but a fixed one when it comes to public speaking. You may have a growth mindset with learning a new language but a fixed mindset with playing tennis. Becoming more self-aware of your mindset in different situations is the first step in recognising how you respond to challenges.

An individual with a growth mindset:

- Sees failure as a learning opportunity

- Seeks feedback to improve

- Is inspired by the success of others

- Embraces challenge and effort

- Perseveres despite obstacles and setbacks

- Considers criticism a valuable tool for personal growth

On the other hand, someone with a fixed mindset:

- Sees failure as proof of inadequacy

- Avoids feedback or sees it as criticism

- Feels threatened by the success of others

- Avoids challenge to protect ego

- Gives up easily when things get hard

- Treats criticism as a personal attack, thereby ignoring valuable feedback

Crucially, the key is not to label yourself as one or the other; it is domain specific. Notice when a fixed mindset creeps in and intentionally shift your focus back to growth. Over time, you will better understand the connection between your beliefs and focus, and the characteristics of growth.

Mindset characteristics

Fixed mindset		Growth mindset
Skills are born	**Beliefs**	Skills are built
You can't learn and grow		You can learn and grow
Performance and outcomes	**Focus**	The process
Not looking bad		Getting better
Keys to growth		
Not necessary	**Effort**	Useful
Not useful		Will lead to growth
Back down and avoid	**Challenges**	Embrace and persevere
Frame as a threat		Frame as an opportunity
Hate them and get discouraged	**Mistakes**	Use them to learn
Try to avoid making them		Treat them as opportunities
Not helpful	**Feedback**	Useful information
Get defensive and take it personally		Appreciate it and use it to grow

As Carol Dweck says: 'In a growth mindset, challenges are exciting rather than threatening. So rather than thinking, "Oh, I'm going to reveal my weaknesses", you say, "Wow, here's a chance to grow".'[26]

The next time you hear someone say, 'I can't draw', remember that this is a belief about a skill. It's a mindset, one they have been taught, but it's incorrect.

To develop a growth mindset in yourself or other people:

- Know about growth mindset. This helps to foster one. Observe your mindset, using some of the questions and frameworks provided in this chapter. Be your own psychologist.

- Mind your language. Words such as 'improve' and 'progress' prime the brain for change and growth.

- Praise others for effort rather than their ability, talent or intelligence. This encourages learning goals and increases motivation.

- Appreciate the power of the word 'yet'. 'I don't know how to knit *yet*.'

Feedback and criticism

A growth mindset views feedback as a gift. The elite performers I have worked with – from the worlds of sport, military, theatre and so on – seek feedback all the time – not for reassurance, but to improve.

However, the vast majority of people in the working world have an issue with feedback. It's something of a taboo subject.

Criticism can understandably sting in any situation – but responses vary. Oversensitivity to criticism can hinder an adaptive response to it, even when it's constructive and intended as helpful, and can develop into fear.

It is possible to learn to respond to criticism in more helpful/less damaging ways by adopting a growth mindset and viewing criticism as an opportunity for personal growth and learning.

How to become more curious

Much of curiosity is about mindset. What does that mean in practice? Here are a few practical pointers:

- **Adopt a beginners' mindset**: In the same way someone might enter a conversation by saying, 'Assume I know nothing' (which may send your conscious mind into an overdrive of possibilities), be deliberately open to and actively looking for new or different ways of doing things. Even if you are highly experienced, approach any new situation as if you are a novice, asking the most basic questions without fear of judgement or appearing ignorant or uninformed.

- **Become a better listener**: Good listening skills help here. Seek first to understand, not to respond. Learn to suspend judgement and resist the urge to explain, defend or jump to conclusions. We will explore listening skills more in Chapter 4.

- **Be truly observant**: Really take in what's happening around you, again without judgement.

- **Be more inquisitive**: One of the best ways to do that is to ask good questions. For example, replace closed questions with more open-ended ones, so 'Did this work?' becomes 'How could this work better?' or 'Why?' becomes 'How come?' Sounds simple, but many people struggle to do this in practice.

In the communications courses I run, I often encourage people to write 'How?' on a Post-it note and pop it somewhere easily visible. Wherever possible, in any conversation, pause, take a breath and try to include the word how in your next question, or turn your statement into a question. In fact, be more Yoda – there is no try! Simply do it.

LEARNING BY IMMERSION

Immersion is a type of research activity performed at an early stage of a strategy or innovation-related project or process. The people directly involved are 'immersed' into their own or related areas of business through carefully planned activities.

Perhaps the best-known example is mystery shopping, in which someone becomes a customer of their own brand or business, but over the years, I've experienced some incredibly creative approaches to immersing a team, from deliberately being late for a flight to causing a scene in a cinema.

The immersion approach is always hugely insightful, often eye-opening, usually memorable and sometimes jaw-dropping. This is because people see, hear and feel the experience in a more visceral way, and observe thanks to the outside-in perspective how others actually make decisions (often irrationally) rather than how they *think* others make decisions.

Actions

- **Use a curiosity prompt**: As part of your journaling practice, write down one thing you were curious about and one thing you learned each day. Every two to four weeks, reflect on your notes and identify potentially recurring themes, patterns and interests.

- **Expand your mind**: Routinely engage with a source, eg a person, a podcast, a community, a talk, an article, outside your typical domain or area of expertise. Write down two to three insights that potentially relate to your strategic work, personally or professionally.

- **Seek new learning**: Find something to learn outside your comfort zone, such as a new skill or idea. To optimise this process, set yourself a clear learning goal at the start.

- **Seek feedback every day**: Don't ask for feedback, just ask for advice. It removes the taboo – and is more forward-looking.

- **Find yourself an accountability buddy**: Use them to assist with all or any of these actions. Look for someone who has different views, beliefs and perspectives to you – providing a good source of 'swaps'.

- **Understand your learning style**: Reflect on two or three of your best, and steepest, learning experiences. What do they have in common?

Key takeaways

- Curiosity is the gateway to strategic insight. It drives open-mindedness and adaptability. The best strategists seek to ask better questions rather than give better answers.

- Curiosity fuels better questions and richer, more meaningful conversations.

- Developing curiosity and individual learning ability is an essential trait of a good strategist.

- Shift your perceptions of learning, removing any sense of compromise. Learning is a continuous activity. Strategic learning is about staying relevant, not being right.

- Learning by doing beats learning by consuming. Learning also involves emotions – stories and mistakes teach us more than facts.

- Learning is about discipline. Prioritise the opportunities to put your learning into practice.

- Grow your curiosity by regularly stepping outside your comfort zone. This is where feedback plays an important role. Learners seek feedback continuously.

- Your ability to change and succeed will be significantly influenced by how fixed your mindset is to growth and learning. A growth mindset underpins lifelong development.

- Learn from your failures and setbacks. Ask yourself, 'What might I do differently next time?' We'll explore this more in Chapter 9 on decision making.

Remember Billie? Billie is curious every day, approaching each task and interaction with an open mind and an eagerness to learn. With her growth mindset, even crises and failures are valuable opportunities to learn and improve.

www.teammandarin.com/
resources/bemorestrategic

4
Be (More) Present, Be A Listener

Good strategists need to be able to converse with many different stakeholders. They filter out biases, assumptions and potentially competing perspectives, extracting the insights and evidence that matter. They also make sense of complexity and uncertainty, constantly looking for patterns, risks and opportunities. A classic example is Mahatma Gandhi, who clearly exhibited all these skills in his lifetime.

Being a good listener will help with all this. It is arguably the most important skill for leaders in any organisation, whether that leader has strategic responsibilities and influence or not.

Many reputable business publications have underscored the critical role of active listening in effective leadership – while also highlighting a prevalent deficiency. A February 2025 article in Forbes, 'The silent superpower', discusses significant gaps in how managers engage in conversations and their listening abilities, leading to missed opportunities.[27] The related research highlights some incredible statistics, including that employees who feel heard are 4.6 times more likely to perform at their best, and that highly engaged teams experience 21% greater profitability, 41% less absenteeism and 59% lower turnover.

However, listening doesn't tend to be prioritised in performance reviews, recruitment or leadership development. These processes are often weighted more in the favour of someone who can speak with authority, clarity and confidence than someone who can listen well, yet I know as a coach and facilitator that it's a skill many leaders need to develop. It may require a few humbling exercises to help them to see just how limited their listening abilities really are.

When I ask any group that I'm working with, 'Who here is a good listener?' at least half usually raise their hands. In fact, despite 96% of people believing themselves to be good listeners, research indicates that individuals retain only half of what others say.[28] When I dig a little deeper and start exploring what good listening really means in practice and, importantly, what it *feels* like from the other side of the fence, people's initial self-assessments are usually swiftly downgraded.

Think about a conversation that you've had recently in which the other person wasn't paying you their full attention. They were distracted in one way or another. How did that make you feel? What did it make you think, both at the time and afterwards? Maybe you weren't that bothered. Maybe you were a little annoyed or frustrated. Maybe you felt disrespected, undervalued or even worthless.

Now reverse the roles and think about a recent conversation where you glanced at your phone, or went into a momentary trance and started daydreaming, or your stomach rumbled and you thought about what you were going to have for lunch. Remember your answer in the first scenario, and there's a good chance that in the second scenario, the person you were in conversation with had exactly the same thoughts and feelings about *you* and, more importantly, about themselves as a result of your actions.

Could and should you be more present in your conversations? Could and should you be more aware of the impact of your own behaviours, however insignificant they may seem to you?

Listening brings its own rewards. A functional MRI study has shown that when we perceive active listening from someone else, it activates the brain's reward system, leading to positive emotional appraisal and enhanced interpersonal interactions.[29]

Listening is, of course, only part of a wider skillset needed to be a great communicator. In other chapters, we'll explore what makes a great question, the value of feedback, constructing and presenting a persuasive argument, and intentions – or underlying motivations – and how these get in the way. However, great listening – and being active in your listening – is such a powerful capability to continually seek to improve. It also plays a key role in being strategic.

It's about empathy and connection. It's about being supportive, building confidence and self-esteem. It's about asking questions that promote discovery and helping to clarify the speaker's thinking rather than simply remaining silent while they talk. It's about being cooperative – allowing a conversation to flow in both directions rather than trying to win an argument.

Barriers to listening

Why is listening well – and being fully present – so hard?

Take a moment to think of one or two conversations that you've had in the last week – maybe one personal (eg at home, with friends and family) and the other professional (eg with colleagues, teachers, customers). At any point during those conversations, were you guilty of doing any of these things?

- Comparing – trying to assess which of you is smarter or more competent.

- Mind reading – second-guessing what the other person really means, not what they are saying.

- Rehearsing – you don't have time to listen, you are too busy preparing your response.

- Filtering – you are listening for something, maybe an anticipated response, or deleting what you don't want to hear.

- Judging – your biases lead you to pre-judge whether or not the other person is worth listening to.

- Dreaming – you're only half-listening, and when something the other person says triggers private associations, you're gone completely.

- Identifying – you are concentrating on relating what you hear to your own experiences and feelings.

- Advising – you like to help and solve problems, so you stop listening and concentrate on searching for the right advice.

- Sparring – you are so quick to argue, debate or put-down that others never feel heard.

- Being right – going to any lengths to avoid being wrong, and refusing to listen to criticism or suggestions.

- Placating – you agree with everything while only half-listening; you get the drift, but are not involved.

- Derailing – changing the subject before the other person has finished.

We all do aspects of these all the time, but in my experience, people recognise what they're prone to doing. For example, many people give or offer advice when perhaps it isn't necessary or hasn't been asked for, or simply isn't the best course of action for that particular person in that particular situation. Because they're busy offering advice – and perhaps thinking about what advice to offer while the person they're with is still explaining their situation – they are not listening, or certainly not listening as well as they might, nor are they as present to the other person as they could and should be. The lightbulb is now over their own head, even though the other person is still talking.

Ask yourself what impact your particular barrier(s) to listening might be having on your conversations and, more importantly, your relationships. In this particular example, over time, the other person might stop coming to you with certain challenges or in particular situations because they simply don't want (your) advice. They just want someone to listen.

Write whichever of the barriers above you are prone to doing on a sticky note and pop it on your laptop or fridge. Simply by constantly reminding yourself of this trait or habit, you will start to shift your behaviour. Better still, tell other people – ask them to flag your barrier up to you whenever you drift into it. The same works for people who umm and err a lot.

Have you ever been told that you finish other people's sentences? Maybe you've been asked not to interrupt someone else mid-sentence. If you are prone to this, practise letting the other person get right to the end of whatever it is they are saying.

To do this, focus on their last three words. Be ready to play back exactly what those three words were – even though you won't actually do this in practice (as that would sound a bit odd). This discipline will create a gap between the other person finishing what they are saying and you responding. You will also create a useful natural silence that they may actually go on to fill – silence is a superpower in its own right – and if they do, keep listening!

The role of the emotions in listening

I've worked with people who have pushed the boundaries of their particular profession to an elite level – everyone from hostage negotiators, professional mediators, military interrogators and fighter pilots to Michelin starred chefs, Olympic gold medallists and World Cup winners. I've heard them explain the value and importance of being a great communicator, and how they learn and continually improve related practices and techniques in their chosen field – as individuals and teams.

They all explain how being a great listener lies at the heart of being a great communicator. I've heard all of them talk about the importance in listening of learning to control and regulate your emotions, one of the Level 1 Deepen Self-Awareness practices. This is neatly explained by what I can only describe as the emotion–cognition see-saw.

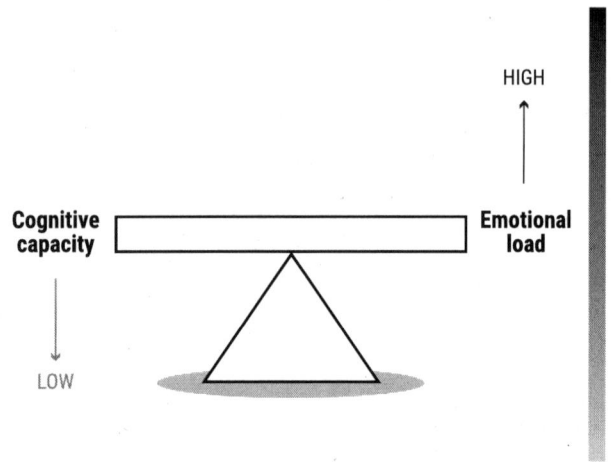

Cognitive capacity and emotional load:
the emotion-cognition see-saw

Remember the amygdala hijack in Chapter 2 – what happens if you're upset or angry. The chances are, you won't be able to focus or think straight. It wouldn't be the best time to wrestle a Sudoku puzzle or perform some algebra.

To use the see-saw analogy, if your emotions rise, your cognitive function or capacity falls. The opposite is also true. Bring your emotions under control (eg through a simple breathing technique such as box breathing), and your cognitive function or capacity will rise.

The see-saw works in reverse. Get your cognitive function engaged in something (eg deliberately and proactively use your memory), and the emotional side of the see-saw will dip.

INHALE, EXHALE

I remember being wired up on a course many years ago so that all my various body and brain functions appeared on screens in front of me. The facilitator then put me through my paces – getting in my face, as the expression goes. Some of the signals went absolutely through the roof – even though I thought I handled it all pretty well, watching it back on video proved otherwise.

Then the facilitator taught me some simple breath work – focusing on my breathing mid-conversation to keep my heart rate steady – and we tried again. This time, he dialled his rage and offensiveness up a few notches, yet using these techniques, I was able to keep my physiology in check.

Watching the second recording back, I realised I was clearly far more able to make sense and listen to what was actually being said rather than what I thought was being said.

If you're able to keep control of your emotions, you will listen more accurately. You will be better able to be present to the other person – no matter the circumstances (think of a hostage negotiator) – and that is likely to help them to keep their emotions in check too. This means they can also listen more effectively and you're far more likely to have a meaningful conversation than two people talking at or over each other.

In a typical conversation, there are usually three elements – and they work in sequence:

- The facts

- The meaning you attach to the facts (ie the story you tell yourself)

- Your reaction (how you respond, ie behave or act)

The key to managing your emotions in a conversational setting is to remember that the middle step – the meaning or story – is your choice. You have control over that choice. And this is absolutely something you can learn to master with practice.

Levels of listening

I often start sessions on leadership, communications or, more specifically, listening by quoting the brilliant book *Time to Think* by Nancy Kline.[30] She famously suggested that the quality of our attention determines the quality of other people's thinking.[31] It's true that non-directive coaching, as it's known, and ego-less listening can and do produce incredible results.

Another author I regularly quote is Stephen Covey, who, in his seminal work *The 7 Habits of Highly Effective People*,[32] stated: 'Most people do not listen with the intent to understand; they listen with the intent to reply.' He went on to say that one of the main aims of asking what matters to us is to help us develop greater intent to listen deeply and understand. In fact, his fifth habit is 'seek first to understand, then to respond'. That's great life advice.

It was through Covey's work that I first discovered the notion of levels of listening.[33] In Covey's view, there are five on a continuum, from ignoring and pretend listening, through selective listening and attentive listening, to empathetic listening – the highest form (ie empathetic listening is key to truly understanding others and creating mutual influence). I remember being really drawn to this, possibly because as someone who grew up in a large family, I often walked around the house wearing a badge that read, 'I'm not deaf, I'm just ignoring you'.

Twenty years on, I discovered the brilliant Otto Scharmer, whose listening model describes four levels: downloading, factual, empathetic and generative.[34] Let me bring this concept to life with a typical example.

Imagine a host or chairperson engaged in small talk at the start of a workshop. As it happens, Billie is attending this workshop. The host asks the assembled group if anyone has been on holiday recently. Billie raises her hand.

The host asks Billie, 'Where did you go?'

'Venice,' Billie replies.

'Ah, I love Venice, I went there last year...' This is Level 1, downloading. The host is waiting to reload. Sound familiar?

Had Billie been the host, she would have been more likely to follow the response with something like, 'Where exactly?', 'Who with?' or 'How was your flight?' This is Level 2 – factual.

Alternatively, she may have asked something like, 'Did you enjoy yourself?' or 'What was your favourite part of the holiday?' This is Level 3 – empathetic. It's all about feelings.

Finally, she may have probed a little deeper: 'Now that you're back, what do you believe you gained from your holiday?' or 'What has it made you reflect on or want to change in your life?' This is Level 4 – generative. She's making meaning out of the responses.

Billie always pays attention to the level at which she is listening. Do the same and you will develop stronger connections and relationships with people, discover more insights, unravel complex issues with greater clarity and make better decisions. This will help you become a better strategist.

EXERCISE: Building your listening muscle

Here are a couple of great exercises you can practise.

Exercise #1:

Find a timer and a partner (or prepare to listen to a section of a podcast or audiobook). Split into A and B (with B being your podcast or audiobook, if required).

A listens to B talk for three minutes (set the timer). No interruptions. Just keep listening, and B, keep talking. Ramble or waffle as required. After three

---

minutes, A plays back an accurate record of what they heard – as best they can.

Do this every day for two weeks. If you find it easy, stretch to fifteen or even thirty minutes.

Exercise #2:

Find a partner and split into A and B. For this, you do need a real human.

A tells B about a problem they're dealing with (eg a work relationship issue). The *only* things B is allowed to say:

- 'And what else?'
- 'Tell me more...'
- 'What I'm hearing is...'

Afterwards, reflect on these questions.

For A:

- Did you want to keep talking?
- Did you feel respected?
- Did you want to share more, and more deeply?

For B:

- What did you notice, as the listener?
- What did this approach allow you to do?
- What role did empathy play?

For leaders who want to capture more data during conversations and meetings, the three levels of listening model by Matt Russell explains what we're listening out for.[35]

- **Level 1 (internal listening)** focuses on our own experiences and opinions in relation to what is being said. While it's important to recognise our internal reactions, emotional responses, triggers and so on, leaders – and others – should minimise their time at this level.

- **Level 2 (focused listening)** is where we listen to the other person intently and curiously, parking our Level 1 thoughts. This is listening to understand or attentive listening, putting our full attention on the person speaking and filtering out our own internal dialogue.

- **Level 3 (global listening)** goes beyond words and encompasses what's unsaid, including facial expressions, body language, voice tone, even silence. This level is profoundly insightful as it helps to shed light on the tone that is communicated and the dynamics at play, especially in a group discussion.

Actions

- **Silence challenge**: In your next conversation, intentionally pause just a few seconds longer than you usually would before responding. You may find that the other person continues to speak so you won't need to respond at all at that particular stage.

- **Reflect**: Practise summarising or playing back what you believe you heard – and understood – before responding.

- **Journal**: After an important meeting or conversation, capture what was actually said (by all parties) and what you believe was meant and/or understood by others.

- **Notice distractions**: Keep track of exactly when and why your mind wanders during conversations – and observe potential patterns and correlations (eg time of day, prior events, mood/ physical state, different people or topics etc).

- **Upgrade a conversation**: Choose one relationship where better listening could really change the dynamic and apply some of the practices from this chapter.

Key takeaways

- Being present – mentally and physically – is essential to being an effective listener, and being an effective listener is key to being a good strategist. It's also a leadership superpower, especially in times of uncertainty.

- Great listeners are rare. Most people listen to respond, not to understand. Poor listening

creates misalignment and missed opportunities,
but listening skills are learnable. They just
require practice.

• Good listeners learn to quieten their inner voice
and suspend judgement. They also learn to better
manage their emotions as these affect how well
we hear and how much we and others share.

• Listening levels vary from ignoring to
empathetic. Deep listening creates trust,
collaboration and insight – which becomes key to
being able to influence others.

Remember Billie? Billie is always aware of the levels
at which she is listening and develops her listening
muscles to build strong relationships, both at work
and in her personal life. This enables her to gain the
maximum for every interaction she enters into.

www.teammandarin.com/
resources/bemorestrategic

5
Be (More) Rational, Be
A Critical Thinker

I f I was to introduce a colleague or friend as an exceptional critical thinker, what would you expect them
to be particularly good at? What would they be like to
work with? How would they come across in a conversation or meeting?

I asked this question recently and the spontaneous
response was, 'Quite irritating because they will be
the person who challenges everything, who asks for
proof, who asks to see all your sources.'

Yep, probably true. Anything else?

'They will ask really good questions.'

Agreed. I see this as a facilitator, moderating workshops or coaching teams. There are normally one or
two people in any group who ask particularly good
probing questions – both of me and of the others in
the room. Crucially, they aren't doing this to show off

or look smart, and the questions are not pre-loaded – they are a natural reflection of the way these people think and process information.

In the early days of writing this book, I pitched to a group of publishers in London. I used this phrase to catch attention – 'The practices, principles and paradoxes of strategic thinking'. It was the word 'paradox' that triggered the most debate from the panel.

The ability to manage paradoxes – apparent contradictions – is part of a strategist's armoury. This helps to highlight the difference between strategic thinking and critical thinking, which often get confused or used interchangeably (like strategy and planning in Chapter 1).

What is a paradox? It is something that on face value seems ridiculous and even contradictory, but is actually true. For example, ever heard someone say, 'Less is more'? This apparently absurd statement means that simplicity or minimalism leads to better results than complexity or excess.

Critical thinking (the ability to be rational and objective, to frame issues, to identify assumptions, to evaluate arguments, all while leaving our emotions to one side) is merely a subset of strategic thinking – albeit an important one. Being a good critical thinker is fundamental to being a good strategist, but be careful not to muddle the two. A strategist needs skills and traits beyond critical thinking, including other types of thinking such as creative, which we'll explore in the next chapter.

Let's return to Professor Roger Martin. The third of his characteristics of strategists outlined in Chapter 3 is 'leverages abductive reasoning'.[36] What does he mean?

Martin explains how 'formal education teaches students two forms of logic':

- Deductive logic – this is taking general principles and using reasoning to reach a specific conclusion. For example, all cars have wheels, a Volvo is a make of car, therefore a Volvo has wheels.

- Inductive logic – this is using data to generate a principle. For example, research states that consumers prefer to download music rather than buy CDs or records, so download speed is the most important metric in their decision making.

So far, so good. This next bit is what really caught my attention, as it explains why strategy is more than just what a spreadsheet says.

Martin states: 'Students are not taught abductive logic, which is the inference to the best explanation – ie what is the most probable conclusion we can reach based on the data at hand.'

He provides a great example: 'My date is checking his/her iPhone all dinner long (data on hand). This date isn't going very well (best explanation).'

Martin goes on to explain how the term 'abductive logic' was coined by the American philosopher Charles Sanders Pierce.[37] He pointed out that you can't use inductive or deductive logic to come up with a new idea – so a third form of logic must exist, which is essential to strategic thinking.

Think about your thinking

This chapter explores what it means to be a critical thinker and provides tools and techniques to do this well. It's also an opportunity to think about your thinking or, more technically, what is referred to as your metacognition – the ability to evaluate your own thinking.

There are ways to assess your metacognition function effectiveness – exploring the alignment between your confidence and actual performance. In one article published by UCL, 'What separates humans from AI?', the author shares their research approach.[38] The method involves participants answering general knowledge questions – for example, 'How high is Mont Blanc?'

Participants rate their confidence in each response. If their confidence is higher when they're correct and lower when they're incorrect, then their metacognition is generally in good shape.

How much time do you spend thinking about your thinking and understanding it? How do you compare your own thinking to other people's? What judgements are you potentially making, possibly unconsciously? Are you thinking – or overthinking?

Have you ever found yourself saying to someone (possibly very quietly), 'Think, just think'? This may have been after something's gone wrong, or is in the process of going wrong, and you're willing them to course correct.

Perhaps you've been on the receiving end of this verbal instruction, been told to think more by a teacher, parent, friend, manager, client or customer. Maybe you've been daydreaming, staring out of the window, and someone has exclaimed, 'Oi, pay attention!'

What happened? Did you become an instant thinking machine?

Of all the people you know and work with, who would you consider to be a good thinker? This might be analytically, creatively or systemically. How might you potentially categorise those around you by their thinking – the quality, excess or lack of it, in your opinion?

Take a moment to reflect on your own thinking style and approach. Identify a few situations in which you know you spent time thinking about something. Was it useful and productive? Were you deliberate and intentional about it? Were you clarifying your existing opinion – or having new thoughts?

What worked for you? What helped or hindered? What might you have done differently?

Of course, in doing this, you may also identify times when you acted too fast – and now recognise that you could have benefitted from spending more time thinking. What might you learn from this? What might you do differently next time?

Let's bring this to life with an example.

STRATEGIC THINKING IN ACTION

The MD of a client organisation is experiencing falling sales. His critical thinking abilities help him to identify the root cause. By having his head up, looking outside-in and analysing the data – employee performance, customer feedback, competitor activity, market trends etc – he discovers that a lesser-known rival has launched a competitive product at a lower price point.

Using a combination of skills, traits and abilities – including but not solely critical thinking skills – he works with his team to brainstorm a range of ideas and options, which they collectively assess and prioritise. The team thinks lowering their own prices is the most obvious and speedy solution, but the CEO recognises, by thinking longer term and reflecting on the company's strategic vision and objectives, that this would potentially trigger a price war and erode any value they've built up over the last three to five years, impacting their brand and future profitability.

Again drawing on a range of skills and traits beyond just critical thinking, the CEO works with his team to design and develop a product differentiation strategy that will help protect the brand and ensure their customers continue to value quality over price (and not get drawn into a race to the bottom). The team works through various scenarios, and ultimately agrees how best to allocate their resources accordingly, focusing on innovation and marketing.

The point is, the CEO and his team have had a moment where good critical thinking was paramount, but other strategic skills were also required (including the soft skills involved in collaborating, which we will explore in Chapter 10).

The CEO also demonstrated two of Roger Martin's characteristics: abductive reasoning and considering multiple variables simultaneously. This led to a decision more beneficial to the wider business than just considering the issue in isolation could have delivered. The CEO no doubt drew on his own experience and intuition too, thereby helping to turn a challenge into an opportunity (in this case, to innovate the company's products and arguably, be more focused in the future).

Thinkers vs doers

People are sometimes categorised – rather simplistically – as either a thinker or a doer. If someone is spending too long on the thinking side of this metaphorical balancing act, people are quick to accuse them – or they accuse themselves – of overthinking.

I've had people close to me say, with good intentions, 'You think too much.' Sometimes they are absolutely right, but on other occasions, from my perspective, I am doing something that they might benefit from learning to do a little more of. That's especially true of people who tend to jump in with two feet; those who act first, think second, and later regret their actions.

In fact, if the outcome of that action is less than desirable, people often say that they should have spent more time thinking about it. I've had countless clients tell me that taking time to think or, better still, learning how to think has been one of the simplest yet most useful shifts they have made as a result of our work together.

A good strategist will balance thinking with acting – situation permitting.

At the opposite end of this (overly simple) spectrum, some people turn the same thoughts or situations over and over in their heads. I often hear people say that they are dwelling on something for too long, not really thinking about it usefully or constructively. Are they simply looking for ways to confirm their own beliefs and assumptions?

This is what people sometimes refer to as overthinking – or possibly ruminating, which in the *Oxford Dictionary of English* attracts two definitions. The first perhaps more technical definition is 'to think deeply'. The second, if you're doing this with other people, is to 'chew the cud'. That's usually a good thing, but many people use the term more negatively, meaning that they find themselves stuck in a thought pattern that continually loops, without ever making progress in the form of a decision or clear next step.

There's an important crossover between this topic and your decision-making style – particularly for perfectionists. We will explore that more in Chapter 9.

When you're faced with a significant decision, how do you differentiate between simply thinking and overthinking? What's the difference? How do you know?

There's a delineation between worrying for the sake of worrying – about something that may never happen etc – and 'Am I overthinking – or just thinking?' Some people believe that because they've taken their time to think something through, they are taking too long to make a decision, they are overthinking.

Many people would benefit from thinking more, full stop. In a course I was running, after the first of four sessions, a senior manager said to the group that her one big takeout was that she simply doesn't think enough. An MD of thirty years said a two-day strategy workshop made her realise that she's forgotten how to think – and she really needs to spend more time doing this sort of work more often, not just when I appear!

It's important to highlight here that just because thinking about something is stressful, that doesn't mean you should stop or avoid thinking about it. In the short term, thinking deliberately and intentionally about a stressful situation can help prompt you into action.

You may have discovered or be on the path to discovering a good balance between taking time to think and taking action. However, if you recognise that your thoughts are unproductive, what might you do?

- **Track your triggers**: Use a journal to keep track of specific events that cause you to overthink. After a period of time, review your notes. You may start to see patterns and be able to develop a suitable coping strategy.

- **Challenge your thoughts**: You do not have to believe what your mind chooses to tell you. Step back – or up onto the balcony (see box) – and view your thoughts and ruminations objectively. What is the evidence? Is the thought logical or helpful? Reframe negative thoughts.

- **Physically move**: Exercise, even if it's a short walk, can help to reframe your thoughts and clear your mind.

- **Experiment with breathing techniques or meditation**: See the previous chapter.

It's important to add that overthinking can be a superpower. You often see this trait in high performers (eg elite sportspeople). People might assume that those at the very top no longer overthink, but that's not the case.

When elite sportspeople are overthinking, they're arguably being vigilant – scanning for potential errors, areas of weakness etc, working through all the different ways things could go wrong. This is where overthinking is a superpower – taking negative material and turning it into a positive force.

If you find yourself overthinking, carve out ten to fifteen minutes to do this more intentionally. Write down each potential scenario and come up with a solution for every single one, because all you need is one more solution than you have potential problems.

Interestingly, we never overthink positive scenarios. We don't get paralysed by worrying about how good something might be. For example, I'm not worrying that this book will be more successful than even my wildest dreams. Humans only overthink negative scenarios. This is the brain trying to control the outcome (control we do not have), not solve a problem. Some argue that the best way to counter overthinking is to start to overthink positive scenarios.

EXERCISE: Balcony skills

There's a concept known as 'adaptive leadership', often compared to technical leadership. The latter is arguably more old-fashioned, based on power and hierarchy.

Adaptive leaders strive to give work back to their people. They know that they don't have all the answers. An adaptive leader must learn to hold tensions (eg between being cost effective and being creative and empowered, between being process-focused and people-focused). They must develop self-awareness – Level 1 of the strategic mastery framework, as described in Chapter 2.

One of the most useful mental constructs used in this work is known as 'balcony skills', which originated in a 2001 *Harvard Business Review* article by Ronald Heifetz and Donald Laurie.[39] The adaptive leader is able to be both down on the dancefloor – among the people – and up on the balcony, able to see everything, including themselves, from a different, higher perspective. Developing balcony skills is equally useful for becoming a better thinker – critical and strategic – especially where you need to be more macro, more objective and/or see the bigger picture.

Take a moment to reflect on a particular issue or challenge that you're currently facing and write it down. A complete, understandable-to-others sentence helps.

> Now visualise yourself walking off that dancefloor and up to the balcony, and looking back down over everything that's happening in and around your issue or challenge.

Framing the issue

Einstein is reputed to have said, 'If I were given one hour to save the planet, I would spend fifty-nine minutes defining the problem and one minute resolving it.' However, people often leap into action having spent not even one minute defining their problem. Leadership teams may dedicate little if any time to agreeing what their most pressing collective issue or challenge is.

One of the most undervalued skills of a strategist is the ability to clearly describe the issue or challenge that their strategy, plan or recommendation is a response to. Put simply, they frame the issue. To be a great strategist, you will need to develop and hone your issue-framing skills. Getting really clear on the issue not only saves you a lot of time, money, energy and other resources, but it also aids communication and decision making enormously. That is why issue framing, as part of critical thinking, is a Level 2 skill alongside learning and listening.

Issue framing is something of an art and a science, and requires certain skills, discipline and practice. It also benefits from a few tools and techniques, which we will cover here.

First, consider the way you naturally think and act. Have you ever solved a problem only to realise that you've created a bigger one? Have you ever spent a lot of time and money on a solution only to later realise that you have fixed a symptom, but not the root cause? This may be true personally or professionally, or both.

A few more questions to ask about your typical approach to problems are:

- Do you tend to dive in two-footed and think later?

- Are you the opposite, sometimes overthinking or getting stuck in thought loops without taking any constructive action?

- Do you simply procrastinate, pushing the problem down the road?

As I approach any problem-solving situation, either on my own or working with a client, before acting or implementing a solution, I think about or encourage others to think about both causes (looking backwards) and consequences (looking forwards). We'll look at causes here, then come back to consequences in Chapter 11 on influencing.

Identifying causes

Consider issue framing in two steps:

- Step 1: Identify and understand problematic symptoms – and separate these from the (root) cause.

- Step 2: Approach the problem from multiple perspectives, helping to reveal biases, blindspots and assumptions. The ability to look at pretty much anything from multiple perspectives is a core skill for strategists.

Let's explore Step 1. Think about a project or initiative you're currently involved in or working on, especially one in which several people are involved. How much time have you spent framing the issue – individually or collectively? If others are involved, how confident are you that you have a shared view of the issue, a sound collective understanding of the root cause rather than the symptoms?

I would estimate that in at least two-thirds of cases, possibly more, the initial issue or challenge that I was asked to resolve was not the issue or challenge that was ultimately focused on. In all those cases, it was a symptom or even a distraction. This was often because the person who issued the brief (the request for help or support) was reacting or responding to something or someone subjectively, emotionally, under pressure and so on. This is in part down to how many organisations are structured, with cultures steering people to act before they have had time to think.

How clearly can you describe the issue or challenge that your plan, strategy or approach is a response to? Write it down. You might find this surprisingly difficult, possibly frustrating, so it could take a few attempts.

Read back over your best attempt. The chances are, you won't have identified the issue. You may have written a goal or the desired outcome, or possibly a potential activity or next step. This is surprisingly common.

Look at what you've written – and ask why repeatedly. 'Why is that an issue?'

If you are working on an issue or challenge collectively with others – have you written the issue down as a team? Before you go any further with your strategy work, it is worth spending good quality time on this. You may discover, especially if you're working in a team, that you identify multiple issues. The chances are there's a correlation and a priority sequence, so ask yourself, is the problem you've presented (which may simply be the one in your head) the problem that really needs to be addressed? Is it the right question to answer first?

The problem statement

This is one of the best tools to help you to get clearer on your problem, and it becomes far more valuable if created as a team via the simple exercise described below. The team might include yourself and at least one other person who has a vested interest in or opinion on your project, initiative, plan or strategy.

EXERCISE: Simple problem statement

Spend five to ten minutes answering these questions:

- What's the ideal (eg desired future state, goals, outcomes, timelines etc)?

- What's the reality (the as-is today, pain points, constraints, insights etc)?

- What are the potential impacts if the problem is not fixed (the consequences in terms of lost time, money, reputation, advantage etc)?

- What are all the options (the possible solutions based on what's known today)?

- What are the assumptions being made and questions to answer next?

Depending on the context, it's useful to include a few simple ratings or assessments for the options, ones that are quick and easy to answer. Examples might include estimated time and/or cost to deliver, the degree of risk, the amount of effort required, the level of confidence to deliver, the degree of complexity (see later in this section) and so on.

If at least two people complete a problem statement for the same problem independently of each other, before sharing their thinking, this stimulates useful conversations using their varying responses to the questions or assessments.

While you spend five to ten minutes responding to the questions presented by the problem statement exercise, the other person/people must do the same, but in isolation. You answer the questions separately, and then share your answers openly and honestly. Explore and discuss your answers – with the aim of creating one single shared problem statement that you are both/all aligned on, one that fairly and accurately reflects all your views and opinions.

I've performed this simple exercise with hundreds of client teams and have never seen two people write exactly the same thing down, even in what might be arguably the most obvious situations. The key is to be clear on your aims and your intent and allow enough time to do this properly.

Again, be aware you may discover more than one issue, which is often why plans and solutions devised without a problem statement don't work as well as hoped or fail completely. In this case, you may need two or possibly three problem statements and a discussion about how you take each of them forward, how they potentially interrelate (eg is one an effect or symptom of another) and which one is the priority.

It can be useful to assess the complexity of different problems, especially when you're making choices between them (eg which to prioritise or allocate resources to etc). At a problem statement level, you might consider whether a problem is complicated or complex. Most people use the terms interchangeably, but there is a clearly defined difference, as explained in the Cynefin Framework:[40]

- Complicated systems often involve multiple interconnected parts, but can be broken down or simplified by removing unnecessary elements or reducing the systems to their essential components.

- Complex systems, on the other hand, are shaped by dynamic relationships and unpredictable patterns. They are difficult to understand or predict because their behaviour is emergent – as are their outcomes – and cannot be reduced to the properties of individual elements. They cannot be explained by examining individual parts alone.

We will explore the subject of managing complexity in later chapters, as being able to manage issues that do not have a single simple solution is an important trait of strategists.

The RED model of critical thinking

The RED model, originally developed by Goodwin Watson and Edward Glaser in the 1920s,[41] remains a great tool for helping us to think critically about a situation, particularly in more structured problem-solving scenarios. It's also useful for highlighting where we might choose to focus our own developmental time and efforts or, if we're working in a team, for those around us.

It has its limitations in that it's quite a linear approach and lacks integration with cognitive biases or more systemic thinking, but it works well as a simple, robust tool to break our thinking down into structured steps. In fact, the Watson-Glaser test still forms the core of many critical thinking assessment tools.

What does RED stand for?

- **Recognise assumptions**: Identify a statement that is implied to be true in the absence of credible proof.

- **Evaluate arguments**: Systematically and objectively assess an assertion intended to sway someone to believe or act in a certain way.

- **Draw conclusions**: Arrive at a solution, decision or recommendation that logically follows from the evidence available at the time.

Let's explore the three stages and what they mean in practice.

1. Recognise assumptions

These two words are fundamental to not only critical thinking, but strategy as a whole – from strategic thinking to strategy development, communication and execution.

A strategy is based on a set of assumptions. We need to work with them to pioneer, to innovate, to be bold and ambitious, to make decisions and progress. Assumptions are fundamental, but of course, they can be dangerous.

Being good at noticing or surfacing assumptions – and better still, challenging them – helps us spot information gaps and potentially flawed or unfounded logic (bearing in mind that strategy creation involves testing the logic of the argument). In an organisational context, whether private or public sector, assumptions are not surfaced – or challenged – nearly enough.

When we're reviewing documents, chairing meetings or listening to pitches or presentations, the underpinning assumptions are rarely shared proactively and upfront. In the written word, such as a strategy document or business case, they're often buried at the back, hidden away in a long list, if they're there at all. In verbal settings, they might be surfaced – and possibly challenged – as the result of a question posed by the audience, but they often just wash over everyone's heads, or people simply choose not to surface or challenge them.

As we'll explore in the Level 3 chapters, you might choose to put your key assumptions at the front of your argument – thereby helping your reader or listener by being really clear from the outset on what you know you are assuming, and what assumptions underpin the message or argument that follows. For example, if you're about to share a recommendation for achieving x and y, let the reader or listener know that this would mean making a decision based on assumption z that you may or may not be able to validate or falsify until point a or b. This can act as a really useful leveller and/or aligner before you dive into detail and assumptions start to whir through the minds of the listeners – either consciously or subconsciously. Of course, in a sales setting, this process is often deliberate, with a good salesperson using their knowledge of cognitive biases to their advantage.

How well known and understood are the assumptions you are making about your current situation – professionally or personally? Have they all been surfaced and, more importantly, challenged?

EXERCISE: Tracking assumptions

Capturing your assumptions from the very start of forming your strategy and simply tracking them as time progresses, once a month or once a quarter, is an excellent way to close the gap between strategy, plans and execution. Everyone writes down all the assumptions that pop into their head or that they're carrying around with them (you and your colleagues can do this alone). Use sticky notes with one assumption per note. Push past the first few minutes and the assumptions will start bubbling up.

It can help to think about the assumptions across different categories or timeframes, for example:

- What assumptions are you making about the future (the next six months, twelve months, three to five years)? What do you assume will be largely the same as today? What will be different, how different and to what degree?

- What assumptions are you making about the external environment – politics, economics,

---

society, environment, technology, regulation – now and in the future?

- What assumptions are you making about the internal environment – relationships, resources, budgets, roles, partners, suppliers – now and in the future?

This exercise is easily adapted for personal life, ie the assumptions underpinning your personal life strategy, your priorities, your decisions and plans.

Once you have all your assumptions out on the table, start to cluster them and identify what feels like it might matter most. Explore why. What's new to you? Where are your potential blindspots? What do you not fully understand?

Take one assumption at a time and question or challenge it. The aim is to identify evidence or data that supports it, ie why you believe it to be true. You're seeking proof. Tangible examples help here, whatever the source.

Does everyone in the team agree? Is there any further supporting evidence or data for that particular assumption? What's the source of this evidence? How credible is the source – and how believable is the evidence?

Now the fun part, especially if you're working in a team.

Invite thoughts on what evidence or data exists that challenges that particular assumption. What do you know or believe that counters the argument? What's the counter-proof? Capture both.

> You may find that you start to surface other underlying assumptions and reveal deeper meaning. You will certainly generate questions that you need to answer – which often lead to the next steps or, in a strategy development process, the work.

I advise my clients to keep tracking their assumptions in this way every month or so – and adjust and amend accordingly. Remember – you might still need to make a decision or take action based on an assumption rather than a fact, but at least you'll be aware that it's an assumption, and will act consciously and proactively, rather than having a blindspot.

This brings us neatly back to the importance of framing the issue and really understanding the cause rather than the effect. To do that, we need to start asking why. Enter Sakichi Toyoda's famous '5 Whys' tool, as used in the Toyota Production System[42] – a simple tool that encourages us to ask 'why?' repeatedly to trace problems to their root cause.

That's basically it. Keep asking why as if you're seven years old again. Kids are much better at this than adults – as we see in other chapters in this book. Adults lose the natural curiosity and creativity they had as children.

Push past the third why, as the magic often resides in the fourth and fifth. Simple, yet so useful. Getting super clear on the issue before anything else will help with all subsequent communication later.

EXERCISE: A simple challenging assumptions exercise for groups

The aim of this exercise is to encourage a group to challenge the assumptions they're potentially making without realising it. It takes the form of what is often called reverse brainstorming.

Pose or identify a problem, eg how can you improve team performance? Instead of solving the problem, which most people will naturally dive into, ask the group to generate ideas for how to worsen it. This is usually quite funny and most people will rise to the occasion.

Discuss what assumptions are behind those 'bad' ideas – as many will mirror real unspoken assumptions held within the team (or wider organisation or ecosystem). Now flip the assumptions – and invite the team to generate new, more insightful ideas and solutions.

2. Evaluate arguments

In a strategic role – and world – you're constantly receiving arguments from colleagues, clients, partners, influencers, politicians – and even your own mind!

These arguments are not always sound. Learning to evaluate them rigorously helps you make better decisions, avoid costly errors and communicate more persuasively. Good strategists don't just listen – they interrogate the logic behind what's being said.

How do you evaluate an argument?

Imagine you're listening to a colleague, a friend, a news anchor or a salesperson presenting you with their views and opinions on a particular issue. If you're tuning into your critical thinking skills, what do you need to do and what do you need to look for?

Ultimately, you need to:

- Analyse the information presented objectively

- Accurately question the quality of the evidence

Put another way, you need to check both the validity of the information (whether it is logically sound, accurate and well supported) and the veracity of the sources (whether they are truthful, credible and reliable). Herein lie two key challenges.

What or whom do we consider a trusted source in an era of mistrust? Where do we go for trusted advice and expertise? How will this continue to change, especially with the rapid development of open-source artificial intelligence (AI)?

The second key challenge here is our own and other people's emotions. How do we make good objective evaluations – and think critically – given that we are ultimately emotional beings?

For example, many people admit to having chosen – consciously or sometimes, with hindsight, rather unconsciously – to avoid potential conflict. They do whatever is required to keep others happy, even if they know, rationally and objectively, that it is a suboptimal choice.

Remember the human iceberg in Chapter 2? So much of what happens – with ourselves and other people – is below the surface.

To evaluate an argument, it helps to have a practical checklist. Try this:

Reflect on a recent meeting or conversation, or listen to someone presenting their case on a podcast or news channel. Even just review a document. Ask yourself five questions:

1. What is the claim? What exactly is being argued? Is it clearly stated or vague?

2. What evidence is provided? Is it data, anecdote, assumption or opinion? Is it sufficient?

3. Is the logic sound? Does the conclusion actually follow from the evidence or are there leaps, false equivalences or gaps?

4. Are the sources credible? Where did the information come from? How reliable, recent or biased might it be?

5. What's not being said? What assumptions, interests or blindspots might be influencing this argument? What alternative views or missing voices should be considered?

Remember, this is not about being cynical or combative, but about improving clarity and decision quality.

In 'recognise assumptions', I suggested a simple sticky note exercise to bring that practice to life. Here's an equivalent for the practice of evaluating arguments using the checklist above.

Imagine a simple scenario involving a return on investment (ROI) claim. Your colleague proposes investing in a new tech platform, saying: 'This tool will save us 30% in resource costs. It's a no-brainer.'

You pause and ask yourself:

- What's the claim? That this tech will reduce costs.

- What's the evidence? Is there actual data? Have pilots been done?

- Is the logic sound? Are the savings guaranteed? What are the risks or dependencies?

- Is the source credible? Who's making this claim? A vendor? Internal tests?

- What's not being said? What about implementation cost, adoption barriers or impact on team culture?

The result? A far better conversation and a far better strategic choice.

3. Draw conclusions

If you've done the R and the E well, D is straightforward.

This is about bringing diverse information together to draw conclusions that logically follow from the evidence available at the time of the decision.

The legendary investor Warren Buffett emphasises the importance of basing conclusions on solid evidence rather than generalisations, and consistently advocates for changing one's stance when new, compelling evidence emerges.[43]

Or, to paraphrase, people who are good at drawing conclusions share two behaviours:

- They do not generalise – they are specific and evidence based.

- They change position when evidence warrants it – they demonstrate intellectual humility and a readiness to walk away from unsupported conclusions.

We will explore this further in Chapter 9 on decision making.

Cognitive barriers

Identifying and mitigating our cognitive barriers – or biases – is key to us developing and improving our critical thinking skills and abilities. First, let's understand some of the terminology before exploring what's actually happening to us, and why.

Heuristics are mental shortcuts that humans use to make quick decisions with limited information. Think 'rules of thumb'. These help to reduce our cognitive load, but lead to biases – errors of judgement – which are sometimes systematic.

A cognitive bias or barrier is a type of bias that arises when we rely on heuristics to make decisions. Put another way, the mental shortcuts lead to predictable errors in thinking. Cognitive biases are primarily there to save the brain time and energy, but they can get in the way of good judgement and decision making. Think of them as shortcuts – as then you can see the benefits as well as the risks.

It can be useful to look at each potential bias related to the problem you wish to solve. For example, what biases might be at play when you are presented with too much information, and yet you need to decide and/or act quickly? This will vary between individuals.

Here are two examples of cognitive biases. They may be unfamiliar, or so obvious that you don't spot them.

Anchoring

Do you have a regular weekly meeting with the same people? Do you produce and/or read a regular report? Every week or month, same format and structure?

Anchoring, the cognitive barrier that may be at play in both these situations, is over-reliance on an initial piece of information – the anchor, even if it's random, irrelevant or wrong. Once that anchor is in place, it pulls our judgement towards it, often without us even realising.

It's a good example of a bias that's everywhere – yet often overlooked. For example, a doctor might anchor on a patient's initial symptoms and miss a more accurate diagnosis later on because the first impression has stuck too firmly. A salary negotiation may start with a figure that's super high – or low – and that number shapes the entire discussion, even if completely unrealistic.

It's also something that we can become more aware of, proactively identifying potential anchors in our day-to-day routines, processes, systems and outlook.

If you have regular meetings with the same people, the best advice is to listen more. Avoid asking leading questions. Make a note of the questions you and others ask and you'll start to see patterns.

Change the agendas. Keep people – yourself included – on their toes. Reverse the order. If you're the chair or facilitator, invite someone else to play that role so that you can listen.

Do the same with those reports – within reason. Does the recipient ever read the last page? Does that matter? If you are the recipient, start at the back. How many final pages did you never reach?

More broadly, think about what sources of information you use to inform a decision or develop a strategy. Think about the last report you read. How much did you challenge it? What other sources of information did you seek?

Over-confidence

Do you ever think you're being over-confident? Are some people around you overestimating their abilities?

The most common version of this is an estimate of the time a task will take: 'Yeah, sure – we'll be ready in a month.' Working in early-stage businesses in particular has taught me that an estimate of one month = three months!

Here are two simple tools to mitigate this particular cognitive barrier. Adopt an outside view – which is good practice for a strategist, per se. For example, take a moment to step outside your own project and learn about similar projects from the past or happening in other industries and sectors. Task yourself with speaking to someone who's been there, got the T-shirt – and listen hard. If time permits, repeat this process with as many examples as possible – and make this part of your ongoing routine.

Perform a pre-mortem – which, for clarity, is not the same as a post-mortem (many people assume it is when they first hear this). A pre-mortem explores the potential paths to failure. This approach helps identify risks at the outset and make the subsequent plan that much stronger. It also helps to sensitise you and your team to pick up early signs of trouble.

Interestingly, this approach reduces the chances of falling foul of another cognitive bias – escalation of commitment, ie refusal to back down from Plan A, even though Plan A clearly isn't working. This is something many of you may have seen or done yourselves. My advice here is to develop Plan B, C, D and E at the outset. As you might hear in military environments, 'fight the fight you're in, not the fight you want to be in'! It makes it far easier to change paths as circumstances dictate.

Adopting multiple perspectives

You are now ready for the second step of framing your issue: approaching the problem from multiple different perspectives, inviting views and opinions from outside your normal circle. This helps you surface and challenge potential assumptions while identifying biases and prejudices.

The principle of outside-in is key to strategic thinking. It's fully explained in Chapter 8 on being future-focused. Here, in critical thinking, being outside-in is about looking in on your problem or challenge – and your assumptions – from a different viewpoint to give you a richer, more rounded perspective.

It's important to proactively seek to recognise those assumptions not only through your own eyes, but through the eyes of various audiences: stakeholders, customers, partners, suppliers etc. Some people do this quite naturally.

Take a moment to think about when and how you do this. What tools and techniques do you use to see things differently? How do you deliberately adopt a different viewpoint or perspective in your professional or personal life?

Perhaps you have experience of helping other people to do this, possibly guiding them to see your own or someone else's point of view. We'll talk more about this in Chapter 11 on influencing and persuasion.

I've always been interested in reading the same news story from multiple different sources, whether they're media companies (newspapers, TV channels etc) or other content providers. This originates from time spent overseas. Reading the same story from different international perspectives sometimes revealed a difference in rhetoric that was quite alarming.

Before you jump to conclusions, learn about the same story from two different sources and perspectives. If you're consuming news articles, make sure you check who the holding company of each source is and that they are indeed separate.

Actions

- **Define a challenge**: Use the problem statement and supporting tools and techniques to clarify a key issue. Ideally, involve other people and invite everyone to populate their own problem statement for the same issue before sharing and discussing your thoughts and responses.

- **Track assumptions**: Write down as many assumptions as you can that you, or others, are potentially making about a particular issue or situation that's important to you right now. Are they true? What evidence do you have? What's the source of that evidence?

- **Practise 5 Whys**: Challenge a surface issue and dig to its core by asking why more regularly (ensuring your intentions are good). Brace yourself – some people might start to find you quite irritating!

- **Apply RED**: Choose a current decision that you need to make and walk through the steps of recognise assumptions, evaluate arguments, draw conclusions.

- **Switch lenses**: Consider your issue or decision from a different perspective (eg that of another stakeholder, customer or critic). Solve a problem from that point of view.

- **Spot biases**: Identify potential biases that are inherent in your processes, systems, routines and/or outlook. How might you mitigate the impact of these biases?

Key takeaways

- Strategy starts with clearly defining the problem or challenge, rather than jumping to potential solutions. A good strategist will frame the issue carefully before proceeding, using their critical thinking skills and abilities.

- Good metacognition – the ability to think about your thinking – provides a strategic edge.

- The RED model – recognise assumptions, evaluate arguments, draw conclusions – provides structure and improves judgement.

- A pre-mortem explores the potential paths to failure, helping identify risks at the outset and make the subsequent plan that much stronger.

- Biases and mental shortcuts distort decisions. Assumptions sabotage clarity – if left unchecked.

- Multiple external perspectives reduce blindspots and sharpen our reasoning, as well as providing key inputs.

- Critical thinking enables better decisions under pressure. Objectivity takes practice – but is learnable.

Remember Billie? Billie's skills as a critical thinker are as helpful in her personal life as they are in her working life. They enable her to remain objective, to identify causes and assumptions, and ultimately, to make better judgements and decisions.

 www.teammandarin.com/resources/bemorestrategic

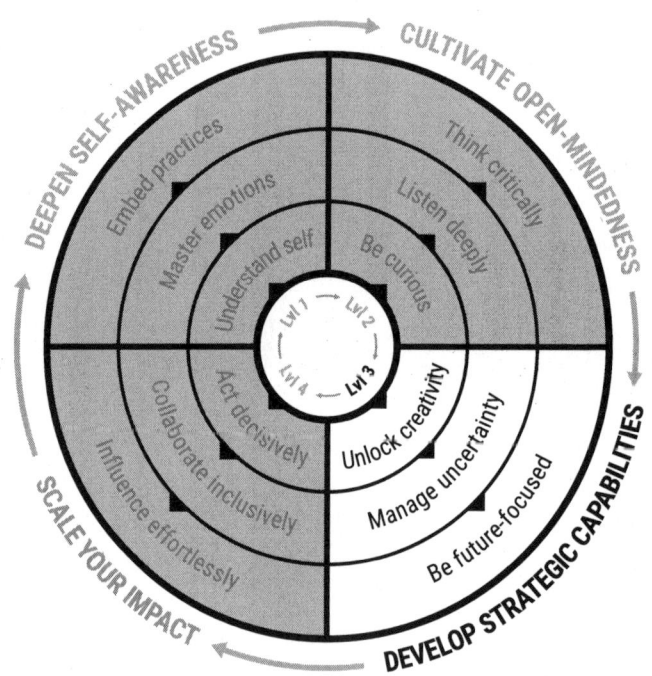

PART THREE
LEVEL 3 PRACTICES – DEVELOP STRATEGIC CAPABILITIES

The practices covered in this section get to the very heart of being (more) strategic. They centre around three concepts that may seem enigmatic to some, possibly baffling to others: creativity, uncertainty and looking into the future. However, there is nothing to fear when you have the strategy mastery framework to hand.

Let's dive into demystifying Level 3.

6

Be (More) Imaginative, Be A Creative

'How can I (learn to) be more creative?'

This is one of the questions I'm frequently asked as a strategist, advisor and leadership coach. The others include 'How can I (learn to) think more strategically?' (see Chapter 1) and 'How can I (learn to) communicate more effectively?' (see Chapter 11), but the creative question is the hardest to pin down.

Creativity is one of the least researched 'fields of expertise', if I can call it that. Perhaps the difficulty in defining exactly what it is (or isn't) explains why.

The leaders and managers I work with are often surprised at just how creative some of what we do in strategy-related projects, workshops and development programmes actually is. For many, strategy is perceived to be about targets and goals, analysis and facts. There is little space for people's more natural intuition and gut instinct, let alone tapping into their creativity and playfulness, or finding solutions beyond the obvious or even from left field.

As we'll explore in a moment, the more analytical left brain dominates the right (we looked at the brain's functions in Chapter 2). That spark of a brilliant idea emerging from someone's unconscious mind in the middle of a workshop will rapidly be suppressed by their own more rational conscious mind – or by someone else's – if it manages to get any air time at all.

I spoke to many people while writing this book who work in what are often referred to as the creative industries – artists, musicians, dancers, comedians, playwrights, improvisation experts, and a former clown, who had similar insights and stories to the various improvisation experts I've met. Several of them mentioned the same challenge: they're asked to help teams and businesses to be more creative, but most managers and leaders a) aren't quite sure where creativity sits or belongs, and b) allow environments to exist where anything even vaguely creative gets killed off before it takes a recognisable shape in someone's head. Many people don't recognise or wildly underestimate just how important the context and environment are, even if you have all the practical tools and skills to be creative.

Greg Hoffman, former chief marketing officer for Nike, shares many brilliant insights in his book *Emotion by Design*.[44] These include how it's important not to leave inspiration to chance. You have to go out and find it, look outside, expand your field of vision to see what is otherwise out of sight, be more curious.

Curiosity, like listening, is a muscle that needs training. Hoffman explains how Nike built a 'culture of creative curiosity' – proactively and deliberately exploring the most unlikely sources, including Space.

In this chapter, we'll look at how you might start to untap your own creativity – making your curiosity more overt, more deliberate, more systemised – and feel more confident and able to come up with new ideas. You can also use what follows to untap the creativity of those around you. With the right conditions, mindset and practices, along with the tools and environment to practise in, creativity can be unlocked in everyone.

The ability to think freely, push boundaries and empathise with others is paramount. Creativity isn't reserved for the select few; it's a skill we can all nurture.

What is creativity?

Let's pause on the word itself – what does creativity mean? What does it mean to you personally?

Do you consider yourself to be a creative person? Who do you perceive to be creative in your own social circles? What about in the public domain? Historically or present day.

To answer the last question, many people will naturally point towards those in certain professions – artists, authors, musicians, painters, sculptors, film directors, accountants maybe...? However, can anyone be creative? I would argue that most people have to be creative on an almost daily basis, to solve a problem, overcome a challenge, get themselves out of a difficult situation, make decisions and so on.

In workshops, I invite people to take a blank sheet of paper and draw out fifteen empty circles in a grid, three by five, ensuring that the circles are large enough to draw in. Next, I tell them, 'When I say start, please draw something *different* in each circle. You have one minute. Start!'

Some people look at me blankly; others look bemused. Some dive straight in and fly through the circles; others put pen to paper, and then pause.

After a minute – or maybe a little longer, just to let people fill in as many circles as possible – I invite them to share their artwork. This usually draws a few laughs, smiles and embarrassed looks. Some hide their work. Typically, people will have filled in most or all of the circles with a combination of symbols, stick men, emoji-style faces and pseudo-hieroglyphics.

I then ask a selection of people to tell me what they actually drew – or tell me about their drawings. They will do so rationally and objectively, talking through what's on the sheet, often circle by circle.

Finally, I invite people to comment on the process and, more specifically, reflect on what they were thinking and feeling, and how they behaved from the moment I gave the initial instructions. This naturally makes them pause and think – I see their eyes moving upwards.

Some might report that the mention of the one-minute deadline triggered a mild sense of panic or fear, which in turn led to something of a brain freeze. Conversely, others might say the opposite, ie the introduction of a deadline helped them to crack on with the task. In innovation work, I often hear people talk about innovation through constraints. A few people will proudly hold up their mad scribbles – clearly having not followed the instructions – and tell me that they don't like rules.

Many people will say, often when prompted, that the later stages of that short timeframe felt different to the earlier stages. Their conscious minds – more analytical, more aware of judgement – started to quieten. On reflection, they realise that they shifted into a state of what is often referred to as flow – a feeling many of us have where we get into something, most likely enjoying it and losing track of time, our more conscious thoughts and the external environment.

Public speaker Jason Silva is credited with saying, 'Flow lives at the intersection of discipline and surrender',[45] the point being discipline and surrender are two elements that help people find flow. Discipline provides structure and focus, while surrender allows people to let go of control and connect with the natural rhythm of an activity.

What gets in the way of being creative?

Imagine a situation in which you are asked to come up with a new idea and submit it by the end of the day. Many people in this situation will suffer a brain freeze; their minds will simply go blank.

What might you do? If you can resist the day-to-day distractions of smartphones, a great technique here is to change your mental channels. Before putting pen to (a blank sheet of) paper, carve out thirty to forty-five minutes and perform a series of short activities in sequence.

For example:

- Go for a ten-minute walk without any technology for company, ie no phones, no music, no podcasts.

- Take a factual book off your shelf (I find non-fiction works better than fiction), turn to a random page and read intensely for ten minutes.

- Put the radio on and listen to five to ten minutes of the dullest broadcast you can find. Shipping forecasts are good – though weirdly fascinating!

- Get hold of some LEGO bricks or equivalent and build something unplanned, or empty a jigsaw out onto a table and see how far you can get in ten minutes.

- For your final ten minutes, allow yourself to simply sit somewhere, free of distractions, hands in front of you, and... get bored. For many people, this is a rare experience. It is also, in its own right, a good form of meditation – just sit and notice your thoughts or focus on your breathing.

MOVE IT!

How do I unlock my creative potential? Move!

Research reveals that even a few minutes of physical activity, such as walking or climbing stairs, can significantly enhance creative thinking. For example, one landmark study from Stanford found that walking increased creative output by approximately 6% compared to sitting.[46]

A more recent study from 2022, known as a 'crossover randomised trial', found that participants who climbed four flights of stairs produced 61% more original ideas on the Alternate-Use Test (a standard measure of divergent thinking) compared to those who used a lift.[47] This was the first formal study to demonstrate that a brief natural stair-climb can significantly enhance everyday idea generation.

By increasing blood flow to the brain, allowing the mind to wander, brief bouts of exercise can help you generate novel ideas and draw innovative connections.

Even simple activities such as walking have been shown to stimulate creative thinking and idea generation. A study at Stanford University found that participants who walked produced twice as many creative responses compared to those who remained seated.[48] Interestingly, the act of walking itself, rather than the environment, was identified as the key factor in boosting creativity.

Being asked to be creative in a group setting brings its own particular challenges. Have you ever been in a situation where you or someone in your group was asked to share an idea? Maybe you or they were encouraged with the words, 'Go on, be creative' or 'Think differently!' What happened?

Usually, there's a lot of umming and erring. As the pressure grows, the inner voices get louder, and any ideas that were starting to emerge go rapidly into hibernation. For many, the fear of judgement and/ or failure rises. (We'll explore the concept of psychological safety more later in this chapter and again in Chapter 10 when looking at collaboration.)

To the earlier example, if you have ever said, 'Go on, tell us a joke', bear in mind that even experienced comedians can find that situation challenging. The point being that we all require time to think critically and creatively.

Challenge your reasoning and beliefs

In the previous chapter, we explored what makes a good critical thinker. Many people define this as the ability to be objective, rational, logical. They put this ability to reason logically into the box defined quite simply as 'thinking'.

As we've explored in other chapters, there is more to thinking than critical thinking. The definition described above is something of a mental model – one shared by many, but no doubt driven by their own beliefs and experiences.

It might be more useful to consider critical thinking – as described above – as critical reasoning. Ultimately, reasoning isn't thinking; reasoning is reasoning. Thinking is far broader and the result of what we might describe as collective reasoning, ie we are processing a problem or situation through multiple different perspectives (and mental models). Hence the repeated emphasis on adopting multiple perspectives not only in critical thinking, but throughout the book.

Let's bring this to life with a few examples. I work with people who are experts in a particular sport. Some choose to commentate on that sport professionally, especially once they have retired from active participation. In that new role, they provide the public with convincing reasoning as to why individual x or team y failed to beat their opponents – but their predictions at the start of the next match are often wayward.

The same is true in other fields. For example, I know journalists who provide commentary on the financial markets. Every day, they share their solid reasoning as to why share prices rise and fall, but they openly admit to not always – or even often – picking the right stocks and shares themselves.

This comes back to assumptions – as explored in the previous chapter – and also beliefs. Beliefs that are often lurking quite far, metaphorically, below the surface of the water in our human icebergs, so we are not even conscious of them.

Think back to the renowned strategist Roger Martin, who is known for his love of the question: 'What would have to be true (for this strategy to work)?'[49] This is brilliant in its simplicity, as it shifts or flips people's perspectives, helping to surface assumptions and make them testable. It's less a question and more of a reframing mechanism, flipping the problem from 'is this strategy right?' to 'under what conditions would this strategy be right?' It's a strategic reframing device that turns guesswork into structured reasoning.

To challenge your own individual reasoning and ensure you're really thinking, and to explore how much of your reasoning is to do with societal beliefs and collective thought, you can borrow from the world of Zen Buddhism and ask yourself a simple question: 'Is that so?' This helps you detach yourself from opinions and social judgements. (The phrase is rooted in a famous Zen story about a monk who responds with only 'Is that so?' when falsely accused of fathering a child. His calm, non-reactive response reflects non-attachment and an ability to remain present.)

For example, a team member states, 'I really want that outcome – but it's going to be incredibly hard to achieve.'

Ask, 'Is that so?'

Your CEO declares, 'We're going to hit the £100 million mark this year!'

Ask, 'Is that so?'

Why does this question help? To the concept of the human iceberg, asking 'Is that so?' allows us to surface and challenge our underlying beliefs.

Go back to the example of the team member above. I hear a lot of people say that to get what they really want in life, they're going to have to go through hardship and suffering. That is what they believe. As a result, they look for every potential struggle and obstacle. Their belief makes them do this to justify suffering as necessary to their achieving what they want in life.

Challenge the belief. 'Is that so? What about all those people who spotted or grabbed hold of opportunities earlier in life than you – and are now ridiculously successful in your eyes?'

'They're just lucky, they somehow cheated the system!'

'Is that so? All of them? What about the person who is extremely content with their life – and has achieved it with little hardship or struggle? We all know at least one of those.'

Silence from most people at this point. Their beliefs are being challenged.

Our belief systems shape our choices – and our decisions. These decisions define the outcomes we experience in life.

We must be careful not to immediately accept collective opinions – or weave them into our judgements and decision making without noticing them. By seeing things outside our current belief system, we can start to make more conscious decisions about how best to shift the direction of our life in a practical, realistic, tangible way. Does everything have to be hard? Do I have to climb every mountain and go through every valley? Maybe not!

Try this out. Go and listen to your favourite speaker, podcast or TED Talk – it must be someone or something you really like, you warm to, that resonates with you. Keep asking, 'Is that so?' in response to everything that's said. Most of the time, whatever you hear and see that you agree with is something you already believe in. It's a cognitive barrier to achieving what you really want to achieve.

Author Julia Galef explores the importance of approaching information with a mindset geared towards seeking truth rather than defending pre-existing beliefs.[50] Galef introduces the concept of the scout mindset in her book of the same name, which involves being open to new information and willing to change one's mind when confronted with evidence.

How to get more creative thinking from others

Many people, even quite senior people in business, admit to hardly ever thinking for themselves. They mostly absorb other people's thinking or delegate their thinking to others.

On reflection, these people tend to admit to basing many of their key life decisions – often subconsciously – on something they once read, or a story they heard, or mirroring the behaviour of someone they admire. They have blindly delegated their own thinking to someone else, and this is what coaching can help them with: having the time – and possibly some guidance and structure – to think for themselves. To work through multiple models and come up with a practical result on the back of their collective reasoning.

Roger Martin's question in Chapter 1 was: 'What would have to be true?'[51] Measured against this, options that would otherwise be shut down by an opinionated opponent get to live longer and there is freedom for creativity. As Chapter 2 explained, whether you consciously feel it or not, when your ideas are challenged, your brain senses a threat. From this position, being creative is almost impossible.

Psychological safety, a precondition for creativity, is the opposite of this. It's the belief that it is safe to speak up and take risks without fear of repercussions or consequences (eg being punished or humiliated). In a genuinely psychologically safe environment – which I believe is quite rare – people feel comfortable to share any ideas, admit mistakes and ask any questions of anyone. They are showing vulnerability, sharing something that someone else could judge.

Certainly in many business settings, most people are somewhat guarded, which unfortunately limits the creative potential of that group. The difference is stark when you spend time in genuinely high-performing environments – usually outside of business.

As we'll explore in Chapter 10, great communicators understand the role of vulnerability in conversations. If both parties are able to share something despite the fact that the other may judge, trust starts to form.

If we can create the conditions for people to feel safe rather than under threat, then there are plenty of ways that we can help ourselves and others to be more creative. We're going to explore a few here.

The power of the unconscious mind

Have you ever slept on a problem? What often happens the next day (or possibly in the middle of the night – which might be less welcome, depending on the problem)?

Maybe you are someone who deliberately goes to bed with a knotty problem unsolved. You are confident enough to say to your friends or colleagues, 'Do you mind if I sleep on it?' People who do this trust the solution – a good idea or the 'right' decision – will come to them with time.

Have you ever lost your keys, your phone or something else that really matters to you? What tends to happen? You retrace your steps. You rack your brain. Someone helpfully asks you, 'Where *exactly* did you lose it?'

For many, the harder they think about it, aimlessly turning over cushions and rifling through the rubbish, the more stressed they become. However, the moment they start to do something else – they get distracted or they have to move on to another task – they suddenly remember where those keys are hanging or that their phone is actually plugged in to charge.

I enjoy reading about the extraordinary lives of great artists, engineers and inventors of the past. Many seemed to be a combination of left and right brained – helping to make them great strategists.

I particularly enjoyed discovering that Thomas Edison, of lightbulb fame, would deliberately fall asleep in front of his log fire with a handful of ball bearings in his hand, which he dangled over a metal bowl. As he drifted into a hypnagogic state (between being awake and asleep), his muscles would relax and the ball bearings would clatter into the bowl and wake him up. At that moment, he would grab his pen and paper (or quill and parchment) and jot down whatever thoughts were floating around his mind. Then, he'd nod off again...

He believed that this technique helped him to capture his most creative ideas from his semi-conscious mind, on the boundary between logic and imagination.[52]

Salvador Dali described using a similar technique with a key and a plate.[53]

And Albert Einstein frequently sailed a small boat on Saranac Lake, not for leisure but to relax deeply and stimulate his thinking. He preferred drifting when the wind died, jotting ideas down in his notebook.[54]

Maybe they were on to something.

THE INNER GAME

You may be familiar with the work of Tim Gallwey and the inner game – Self 1 and Self 2.[55] A great example of how this works is in teaching young children to catch and build confidence in their catching.

Simply grab a selection of tennis balls of different makes or colours, depending on the age of the child/ what's available. As you throw the balls to the child, ask them to call out the colour/brand. Self 1 – their conscious mind, which could hold them back with inner criticism – focuses on answering the question, while the unconscious mind – Self 2 – ensures the body moves as needed to catch the balls.

Play and delay

In the 1960s, a landmark study was conducted in the United States into what made particular architects so outstandingly creative.[56] Why architects? Because they need to strike a balance between being super creative and super practical. Clearly, some are more creative than others – just look around your nearest town or city.

The study discovered two key differences between the most creative architects and the least creative. The first difference is that the most creative know how – and when – to delay. If a key decision isn't required until next Friday, then they will happily wait until that time to give their decision.

Hang on. Doesn't that simply mean they are indecisive? No, far from it.

The psychologist who conducted the study, Donald MacKinnon, discovered that this particular group had learned to trust that with more time for subconscious thought, and to glean new ideas and insights, the best possible ideas, and therefore the best possible decision, would emerge. He went on to say that it's discomfort with the uncertainty of not having made a decision (yet) that causes many people to decide early, without ever knowing if a better, bolder idea or decision was just around the corner.

When you're faced with a significant decision, do you delay? Do you procrastinate? Most people do at some point – we'll explore procrastination in depth in Chapter 9 – but are you a serial procrastinator? In my experience, a few people will admit to this, usually with a knowing smile.

Now let me ask you a slightly different question. Are you the sort of person who knows there is something on your to-do list requiring a decision – it's not necessarily the most urgent or important or difficult, but simply knowing it's there means you push it up to the top of the priority list – and you decide, swiftly? You tick it off.

The organisational psychologist, Adam Grant, popularises a concept in his TED Talk.[57] He describes procrastinators as 'instant gratification monkeys' and pre-crastinators as 'panic monsters', terms coined by Tim Urban, creator of the blog Wait But Why.[58] Peak creativity sits somewhere in the middle of the two.

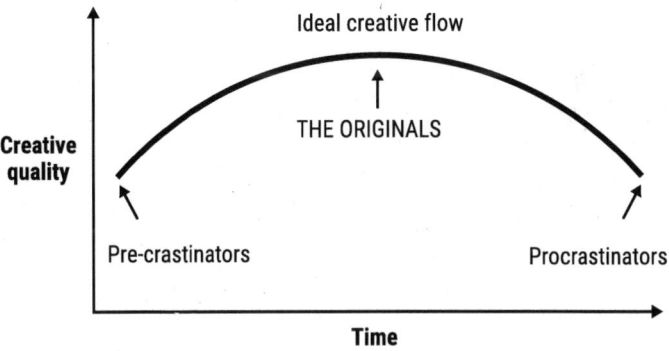

Graph to show the ideal creative flow

The second difference the study found is that the more creative architects know how to play. They deliberately use their working hours – as well as their personal time – to experiment, to learn, to be exposed to new challenges, perspectives and stimuli.

Peter Skillman, a design thinker, devised a challenge that pitted young children against CEOs and MBA students to build the tallest possible tower in twenty minutes out of nothing but pasta, marshmallows, tape and some string.[59] Guess who built the largest tower? The children. Followed by the CEOs. In last place, the MBA students.

Kids play. They just pile in. They experiment, they test and learn. This includes sticking pieces of pasta up their noses. They don't plan. They push through the phase of uncertainty and ambiguity without worrying about the result and/or attempting to figure out the answer before picking up the first marshmallow.

There are no aims for children. There are no rules. As far as we know, especially for the youngest children, there is no consideration for what others think. Compare that to the underlying fear that ripples around many a boardroom.

LEGO Serious Play® is an increasingly popular technique that I have used in hundreds of workshops around the world, often attracting strange looks from customs officers at airports: 'Why so much LEGO, sir?' It is a structured hands-on approach that helps to solve complex problems and build futures, and in so doing, it enhances creativity and teamwork. It originated in the 1990s from research at the IMD Business

School in Lausanne, Switzerland, and was later developed by LEGO.[60]

It works by engaging participants in building models, storytelling and reflection, fostering deeper thinking and collaboration. The method is effective because it leverages play to unlock new perspectives, encouraging open communication, and taps into subconscious insights, making problem solving more engaging and innovative.

I've used this technique, and variants of it, hundreds of times, in many different situations. I've worked with people one to one, and once ran a single session with 180 people – now that's a lot of LEGO! Despite a few huffs and puffs (exhaling for effect) and exclamations of, 'Our CEO will never do this!', most quickly lose their inhibitions. They stop thinking so much about what they are doing and what others might think – and they build. They play.

Keep iterating!

This is such a simple idea, but it touches on and ties together so many other strands described in this book (eg listening, learning, thinking, decision making etc).

First, let's clarify what we mean by iteration. The *Oxford Dictionary of English* will tell you that iteration is 'The action of repeating something, typically a process or set of instructions'. In a creativity context, what's important is that those outcomes are potentially unbounded – if you follow the processes accurately and, of course, have the right conditions in place.

EXERCISE: Iteration games

Remember the circles exercise I described? There is a variant of this exercise in which I ask people to draw their first idea in the top left circle (eg a symbol, an emoji, an inanimate object) – and then rapidly iterate it in every subsequent circle over the space of a few minutes to see what emerges.

This is similar to another brilliant exercise that originates from the design world and is commonly referred to as Crazy 8s. Here, you and your team take a sheet of A3 paper and fold it or score it to create eight similar sized boxes. This is your canvas.

Working individually, everyone takes their best idea, which is often in written form, and spends no more than sixty seconds drawing this idea in the top left box. As you hit the sixty second mark – so entering minute two – everyone moves across to the second box and draws a different version of their first drawing. After a further sixty seconds, regardless of where people are at with their work, they move on again – and repeat the process until all eight boxes have something drawn inside them (or not, in some cases!).

Most people struggle at the start, but quickly find their flow, and the room starts to go really quiet by about box three or four. At the end, most people are pleasantly surprised by their outcomes, which tend to fall into one of two camps: some are remarkably similar to the first drawing, even though the middle drawings have deviated significantly(!);

others end up with something completely unrecognisable but rather brilliant in Box 8.

Oh, and nearly everyone is likely to comment on how exhausting the process is.

You may have unintentionally tested the iteration theory if you have ever had the misfortune to be nearing the end of an important document (eg a proposal or presentation) – only hours before the deadline – when disaster strikes, your laptop dies and you lose your precious work. What happens? Perhaps after a mild panic and some choice language, you either give up or create a new version – from scratch. All the time, though, you're thinking, 'Ah, but my original was so good, I'll never remember what I wrote, this version will be terrible.'

Does it turn out that way?

This exact thing happened to me while I was writing this chapter on a train with no internet connection. I took a deep breath and started again. When I finally returned to my desk, I was somehow able to retrieve a version of what had existed shortly before my laptop's partial retirement and compare the two versions. The second version was infinitely better than the first – more insightful, more succinct.

From a strategy point of view (thinking, development, refinement, communication), these three practices – trusting the unconscious mind, play and delay,

and keep iterating – are key. There is certainly something of a paradox between these practices and the
more objective, rational, analytical attributes we often
think about when exploring all things strategy, but in
developing your creative muscle, you will improve
your strategic capabilities.

Actions

- **Immerse yourself**: Explore a new (or not so
  new) world by immersing yourself first-hand.
  Identify examples of organisations that share the
  same issues as your own – even though these
  might not be so obvious on the surface. This is a
  great way to gain insight, challenge your beliefs
  and assumptions, and be inspired.

- **Build stories**: Facilitate a LEGO Serious Play
  session to help unlock a problem or generate
  new ideas (eg for a marketing campaign).
  Simply start by building the story and let the
  ideas emerge.

- **Schedule play time**: Allocate thirty to sixty
  minutes per week for free-thinking time without
  any deadlines or deliverables.

- **Question beliefs**: Experiment with some of the
  relevant questioning techniques provided in

this book, such as 'Yes, and…'* or asking 'What would have to be true?' for a challenge you're facing.

Key takeaways

- Creativity is a critical skill for any strategist, one that we can all learn to do more and better. It is not a mystical talent.

- Everyone has creative potential – it's about unlocking it rather than manufacturing it. Being able to unlock the creative potential of others and provide the conditions for creativity to flourish is another thing we can all learn and practise.

- Creativity as a strategist includes divergent thinking, scenario planning and idea generation. Creativity also supports visioning and problem solving.

- Creativity is influenced and supported by the environment and by emotional safety – so give both due consideration.

---

*   A powerful tool from the world of improv is a simple phrase: 'Yes, and…'. At its heart, this technique is about accepting what someone else has offered ('yes') and then building on it ('and…'). It encourages openness, curiosity and momentum, which are all essential ingredients for creative thinking. In workshops, using 'Yes, and…' can transform a conversation from cautious and critical to bold and generative. It doesn't mean agreeing with everything, it means suspending judgement just long enough to explore where an idea could lead.

- Play, improvisation and curiosity fuel imagination, and imagination allows you to think bigger, deeper and wider.

Remember Billie? Billie never misses an opportunity to flex her creative muscle, and she ensures her team has a safe environment to develop their own creativity. She listens to and respects all ideas, knowing that the best solutions often come from the wildest flights of fancy. Furthermore, Billie has never forgotten the freedom of expression she enjoyed as a child. Billie plays regularly, and her team loves to play too. She just needs to make sure she doesn't spend too long with her LEGO set!

www.teammandarin.com/
resources/bemorestrategic

7
Be (More) Comfortable With Uncertainty

During the Covid pandemic, the number of people I engaged with day-to-day went up tenfold. In the first six months or so, between March and October 2020, I ran a virtual workshop or facilitated some form of group interaction with over 3,000 people in more than twenty countries. In addition, I continued to act as an advisor and coach to twenty-five+ leaders across a variety of organisations – all while trying to home school my children.

I remember noticing as the months ticked by, and the lockdowns came and went, how incredibly varied people's responses were to this sudden craziness. Aside from the actual pandemic and its terrible, devastating consequences, every facet of people's day-to-day lives was suddenly being thrown up in the air with no real sense of when they were going to land – or where – or if they would at all. The sense of uncertainty and ambiguity was profound.

In March 2020, I had multiple overseas trips scheduled to destinations including China, Russia, India, Poland, Portugal, the UAE and the Philippines. As the dates grew closer, I noticed a clear gulf in how different people in different locations decided whether we would continue as planned, delay or defer, cancel outright or shift the sessions online. How people managed the uncertainty varied enormously – and there wasn't any obvious correlation between who did it well vs less well and their age, experience, role or background.

The notion of managing uncertainty, and how comfortable people are – or not – with things being uncertain or ambiguous (or unplanned) and not being in (full) control, is something that's always fascinated me. Comfort with uncertainty is a key characteristic of being a good strategist – something we see through military and geopolitical history, from Sun Tzu's *The Art of War*, which is essentially a guide to thriving in uncertain conditions, to the Prussian Carl von Clausewitz, who introduced the concept of 'fog of war', the idea being that in battle, uncertainty is the norm, to modern business leaders such as Andy Grove of Intel, who famously said, 'Only the paranoid survive',[61] and Jeff Bezos of Amazon, who operates with a ten to twenty-year time horizon, but encourages a Day 1 mindset that embraces uncertainty. Being comfortable with uncertainty is as relevant to us in our personal lives as it is in our professional ones.

The good news is we can all develop these skills and attributes.

You need not only the right tools and techniques, but also the right mindset (eg choose your mood, feeling the fear) and practices (eg rituals, routines, habits). You need a strategy (not a plan), which as you know from Chapter 1 can make you more rather than less anxious.

Upskilling people in how to manage ambiguity and uncertainty is crucial. It is key, for example, to being a good leader because it helps you create the conditions for innovation to flourish, and for people to feel empowered and thrive. On a more personal level, it helps you to manage your own wellbeing and, ultimately, prevent burnout.

The problem with uncertainty

Many people struggle with this issue. They aren't aware of their propensity or attitude towards uncertain situations, and many leaders are not aware of the skills and attributes that, certainly in a professional context, they would benefit from developing.

How does this play out? As we discussed in Chapter 3, many organisations have leaders who are continuing to manage. They can feel great discomfort in unpredictable situations, where they can't control what's happening around them. As the Stoic philosopher Epictetus observed, 'Some things are within our power, while others are not.'

Managing uncertainty involves two different sources of psychological stress (or what researchers call 'key stressors in uncertain situations'):[62] unpredictability (you don't know what will happen) and lack of control (you can't influence what happens).

On the whole, people handle things better if they can see them coming and believe that they have a degree of control over them. Without that being the case, their fight-flight-freeze response (see Chapter 2) kicks in – and everything starts to go a little pear-shaped.

People often benefit from simply learning to control the controllables – to focus their efforts and energies only on what they can control and potentially influence, making the best decisions that they can with the information they have at that time.

I've consulted on many change programmes – transformation projects across large teams, functions and divisions, or even entire organisations. There is usually an element of people feeling fearful of the upcoming changes and what these might mean for them personally – from no longer sitting next to a good friend or in that great spot by the window, to losing their job, their livelihood and, for some, their identity.

Increasingly, beyond working on the content of the change (eg the strategic direction, the future business model etc), I have worked closely with the leadership teams and those that report into them on how they manage the uncertainty or the change. Much of that is about developing the right mindset and adopting useful practices.

As a strategist and a coach, I regularly explore how different people respond to uncertainty, ambiguity or the unknown. As humans, the way we self-manage under stress often reveals our more deep-rooted belief systems – highlighting how we've learned to make sense of the world around us.

Ask yourself – what is your default behaviour in times of great uncertainty? How does this default behaviour help or hinder your thoughts and decisions?

The chances are, your own default behaviour will fall into one of three reactive tendencies: complying, controlling and protecting. As fellow Leadership Circle practitioner Paul Byrne explained, 'These aren't flaws. They're echoes of an earlier meaning-making system – adaptive strategy often shapes in childhood to help us manage anxiety, navigate relationships, and stay safe in a world we don't yet understand.'

Karen Horney, the brilliant psychoanalyst, described these tendencies as three basic responses to anxiety in her well-known theory of neurotic needs and coping strategies:[63]

- Moving towards others – or complying – ie seeking connection, harmony and approval (compliant type).

- Moving against others – or controlling – ie asserting strength, influence or competence (aggressive type).

- Moving away from others – or protecting – ie withdrawing into independence, caution or self-sufficiency (detached type).

These are also known as the three basic interpersonal orientations.

As a Leadership Circle practitioner, I work with leaders, both experienced and emerging, to explore how their own default behaviours – especially in times of uncertainty – enable or limit their leadership impact and effectiveness.

It's important to explain that the three responses above are all perfectly natural, but as Paul points out, they can become overused, especially in the complex environments of senior leadership, limiting our choices. They're not problems to fix – they're signals to explore.

Ask yourself – when might your go-to move under pressure be getting in your way? Here's what I advise.

Train your brain

To do this, you need to understand what's happening in your own and other people's brains.

In times of uncertainty, it's normal for us to struggle with a negative bias where a degree of cynicism tells us that ambiguous situations must contain a threat. In fact, ambiguity often precedes meaningful breakthroughs and new possibilities, so encourage a healthy scepticism or a realistic optimism that allows you to remain open to potential benefits and creative learning. Again, this is as true in a personal capacity as it is in a professional one.

Realistic optimism is a form of positive thinking, though it's a little different to the usual definitions. It is about believing that you will succeed and having a positive outlook, while acknowledging the work required and the difficulties you may encounter.

Let's go back to the simple brain science, as it helps with this explanation. During periods of change and uncertainty, many people feel under threat – possibly subconsciously. Sensing that threat, our brain helpfully starts to shift us downstairs, preparing the body to act.

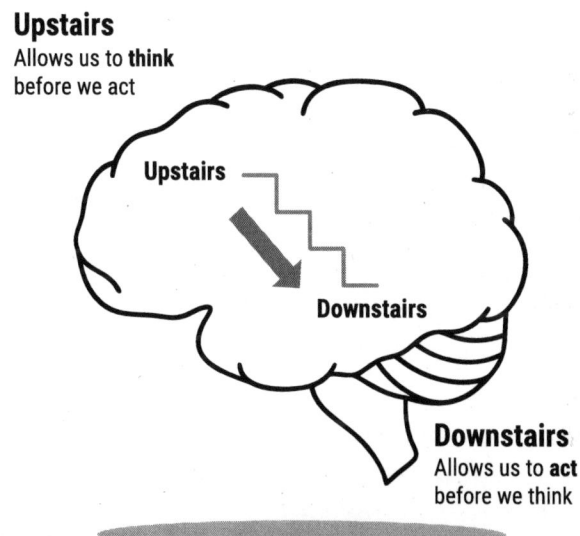

Upstairs
Allows us to **think** before we act

Upstairs

Downstairs

Downstairs
Allows us to **act** before we think

Upstairs vs downstairs brain

Understanding your natural response to uncertainty offers a valuable window into how you lead, make decisions and relate to others, especially when the stakes feel higher than normal. By recognising these patterns and pairing them with a mindset of realistic optimism, you're not just managing ambiguity, you're using it as a space for growth and leadership.

The ability to remain steady, curious and grounded in uncertain times is what enables leaders to unlock new possibilities, for themselves and for those around them. Being a realistic optimist isn't naïve, it's strategic. It's what allows you to face difficulties with clarity and composure, respond with a positive intent and lead with courage, care and compassion.

Understand – and use – the change curve

Many people – especially in large organisations – will have heard of this concept. You'll possibly recognise its form, but it's often misunderstood.

It's a simple model that describes the stages most people go through as they adjust to change. Though popular in organisations, it's actually created by psychiatrist Elisabeth Kübler-Ross, resulting from her work on personal transition in grief and bereavement.[64] Importantly, by way of context, Kübler-Ross explains it's 'change that has been forced upon us not that we have chosen for ourselves' that triggers the grief response.

The change curve is useful for helping people to manage change and uncertainty – in their work or with other people. For example, it gives everyone a shared language – which in itself is incredibly helpful – and links to over-communication, which is described later.

I tend to use the Kübler-Ross model (ie the three levels on the horizontal axis of the change curve[65]) as the basis of four broad stages of my own.

They're not meant to replace the original, rather to help you think about what's happening to you, your team, your family etc during change. My stages are:

Stage 1 – Status quo: Life feels as it did before the change. We hold on to what's familiar, ask questions and seek clarity.

Stage 2 – Disruption: Things become uncomfortable or stressful. Fear, frustration or resistance may arise as we begin to process the impact of change.

Stage 3 – Exploration: We start testing, learning and making sense of the new reality, experimenting with ways to adapt. We may occasionally slip back into disruption as we do this.

Stage 4 – Rebuilding: We integrate and accept the change, rebuild our norms and begin to see the benefits, becoming productive and confident again.

Different models will group or label these stages differently. The key point is not the names, but the pattern and the realisation that change is emotional as well as practical.

Here are a few pointers. The curve is, of course, non-linear. We shift rapidly and continuously, back and forth along it.

Think about when the pandemic struck. You no doubt bounced around the curve as the news broke, announcements were made, rules were set and changed. You were managing multiple curves simultaneously.

With a major change at work, you're aware that within it, you might have new bosses, colleagues and offices, which means your commute might also change. Meanwhile, it could be that your parents are unwell, your utility bills are rising, your car is constantly breaking down, your...

Tiring, right?

This is why it's so important to develop good routines, habits and practices. With times of uncertainty, there are four I recommend:

- Every day, ask yourself – what did I learn today?

- Proactively manage your energy. What gives you an energy boost (seek more of this, more often) and what's an energy drain (avoid/limit this)?

- Take control (see Stephen Covey's circle of influence below).

- Develop rituals of recovery – the highest performers recognise the value of rest.

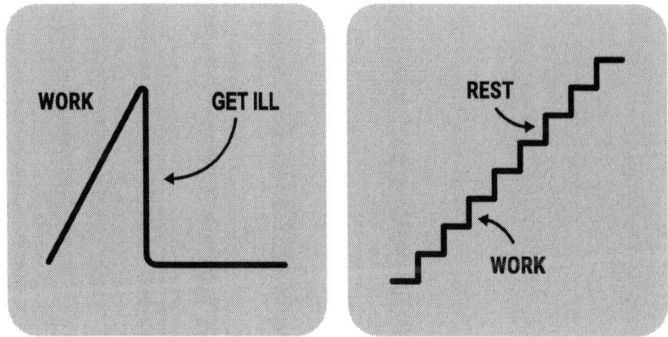

Pick your path

EXERCISE: Plotting where you are

This exercise is intended for two to four people.

Grab a pen and paper each and sketch the change curve from the website mentioned. This helps you to familiarise yourself with the various stages.

Each person plots where they sit on the curve right now, potentially noticing that they might be in multiple stages at once, depending on the context/ topic etc. Invite everyone to share with each other – openly and honestly – where they are now, where they may have been in the recent past and what's potentially moved them (eg passage of time, a discussion with someone etc). Explore some of the differences and similarities in the group.

If useful, repeat this exercise again – a week/ month later – and use the language of the curve in conversations outside of this exercise.

Communicate, communicate, communicate!

Over-communication, especially in times of uncertainty, is key, otherwise fears can fester/amplify. I'm talking daily, if not more. If you're a leader, it'll pretty much be your only job.

A CEO whose company was starting a huge organisational transformation asked his team if they wanted to see his notes in preparation for their meeting (ie see what he had written down about his own fears). Intrigued, they agreed. The CEO walked over to a flip chart and unveiled not one, but three entire sheets covered in his fears about what was to come.

This one brave action completely changed the nature of the conversation in the leadership team. Why? Among other reasons, the CEO was communicating openly and honestly. It was a great example of showing vulnerability too.

In Edward Berger's 2024 film *Conclave*,[66] adapted from Robert Harris's novel about the election of a new Pope, Ralph Fiennes plays – rather brilliantly – the character of Thomas, Cardinal Lawrence, the Dean of the College of Cardinals. Cardinal Lawrence is responsible for managing the election with all the Cardinals sequestered from the outside world – no easy task.

On the first day of the Conclave, he delivers an intuitive sermon on the value of doubt. 'If there was only certainty and no doubt, there would be no mystery and therefore no need for faith,' he says.

He is somewhat impartially encouraging the Cardinals to accept that for the Church to modernise, it must be open to change. They should therefore question and possibly challenge existing rules and beliefs, and vote accordingly (ie for the more liberal candidate).

He states that certainty is opposed to unity, tolerance and mystery. This is well worth communicating to your team.

Perfectionism and uncertainty

I worked on the strategic creation of a learning culture within a global organisation – no small task! In one session, I was describing some of my own personal learnings from working in elite high-performance environments.

One participant – quite understandably – asked: 'Charlie, what can we possibly learn from these people? They are close to perfect!'

My response was – and the point is – that in true elite teams, where the stakes are incredibly high, a culture is embraced by everyone involved that recognises we cannot always get it right. In fact, the culture understands that we need to make errors to improve and learn as quickly as possible. Therefore, elite teams are great examples of environments in which the individuals and system continuously test, experiment, learn and grow. They certainly don't see themselves as perfect.

It's important to accept that in ambiguous situations, rigid plans will quickly become obsolete. You will never have perfect information for your decision, so embrace a degree of flexibility by adapting and adjusting your strategy and your plan as new information emerges (as a result of the action you have taken).

As we'll discover in Chapter 9 on decision making, there's a clear link between how someone manages uncertainty and their decision-making style – especially when under pressure. For example, if you are something of a perfectionist, you will struggle with times of uncertainty and ambiguity because, by their very nature, they require experimentation and iteration. You need to take a few calculated risks, try out those ideas and learn from your failures (as discussed in the growth mindset section of Chapter 3).

Many people I work with would put discomfort with uncertainty as one of their more pressing challenges or possibly weaknesses. Life can be uncertain, and then our normal responses and coping strategies simply don't work. People tend to love a good routine or need to feel in control of their circumstances and always have a plan, so when they're hit with unknowns, ambiguity, unpredictable events or things not turning out as expected, they struggle. In fact, many would say that they no longer feel safe (think of the human iceberg).

This is certainly something that we can develop and shift. As professor of psychology Elaine Fox says in her book *Switch Craft*,[67] we need to cultivate our mental agility – a nimbleness in how we think, feel and behave that will allow us to adapt to changing circumstances. The more psychologically flexible (or mentally agile) we are, the greater our wellbeing tends to be, and the less vulnerable we are to anxiety and stress.

People who dislike uncertainty are often life's worriers, because worrying gives them a sense of control in a difficult situation (at least they're doing something). This is a cycle they need to break. Otherwise, they might shy away from challenges that they could fail at – which links to what we'll explore in Chapter 9 on decision making. They are afraid of getting things wrong and expend vast amounts of energy on thinking through decisions – without ever actually deciding anything.

Navigating uncertainty

We live in what strategists love to refer to as a volatile, uncertain, complex and ambiguous (VUCA) world. Adapted from the US military, the term has now become mainstream in business to describe the context and environment within which leaders need to operate and make decisions.

Again, we refer back to Chapter 2 on self-awareness. Leaders need to know how to use and understand their strengths, including their values and beliefs, to better inform how they lead and manage others, and improve the performance of their teams and organisations – authentically and sustainably. They need to do all this in a VUCA world.

I love to use this exercise when working with people to improve their strategic thinking skills. Here's how the conversation might go. I'll ask who in the group is one of life's planners. Likes to plan everything in a social situation. Loves a list. Maybe even has a list of their lists.

Then I'll probe a little further and ask who likes to be in control. This second group is usually a small sub-set of the first group.

I show the group this image, and ask people how it makes them feel and where they would place themselves.

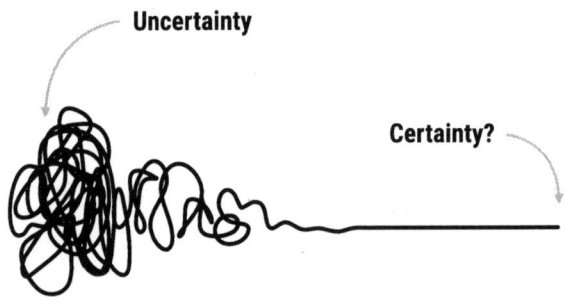

Uncertainty vs certainty

People who are uncomfortable with uncertainty – normally my planners and my self-confessed control freaks (their words, not mine) – have a strong reaction to the more squiggly side of the image above. They might admit to making too many to-do lists, over-preparing unnecessarily and becoming disproportionately anxious when plans or circumstances change.

Here are a few tips to help them – and you – navigate uncertainty:

Embrace flexibility

Plans are important, but being able to adapt when things don't go as expected is even more critical. Journaling will help you to become more conscious of your thoughts, feelings and behaviours through any unexpected – yet inevitable – changes.

Focus your energy on what you can control or influence

There will always be variables outside your sphere of influence, so concentrate solely on what you do have control over.

In Stephen Covey's brilliant book *The 7 Habits of Highly Effective People*,[68] the first habit is 'being proactive'. This is about believing that we are in charge.

As Covey points out, what distinguishes us as humans from all other animals is our inherent ability to examine our own character, to decide how to view ourselves and our situations, and to control our effectiveness. Put simply, to be effective, one must be proactive.

Covey goes on to explain that we all have our own 'circle of influence' (things we can affect or change) and 'circle of concern' (things we can't). You may have heard these phrases, but often, people don't know much more about them or how to apply them in practice.

I use variants of this idea all the time: in my personal and professional life, in more strategic contexts (as we'll explore in Chapter 11 on influence), and in coaching situations. It's especially true for people managing periods of change or uncertainty.

If anything is outside of your direct control or influence, make a note of it, then park it until the following week/month. Avoid ruminating!

Build resilience over time

Squaring up to and proactively taking on a series of small challenges or uncertain situations (eg opening yourself up to questions or facilitating a conversation rather than simply presenting information) can enable you to build the confidence to deal with bigger challenges further down the line. Again, journaling will help here, paying particular attention to your values, beliefs and fears.

Trust your unconscious mind

The 'right' decision, solution or approach – especially in VUCA circumstances – is unlikely to appear overnight. A good strategy development process will be drawn out over a series of sessions/weeks by design. As we learned in Chapter 6 on creativity, we must trust in the process and the time it takes. Involve different voices and opinions. Clarity will appear. As my friend, mentor and former boss Charlie Dawson would say, 'Let the lights emerge through the fog.'

I recently shared these insights – along with the squiggly line image – on a strategic skills programme I was leading. I asked people to reveal how far to the left (the squiggly side) they had to be to start feeling uncomfortable, ie when they no longer had control of what was happening around them and/or when they were managing or leading a team in uncertain, ambiguous circumstances. One attendee told me that this image, especially how far to the right she placed herself, really struck her and led to her having several in-depth conversations with her husband. She realised just how uncomfortable with uncertainty she was and recognised the need to prioritise this development work.

Moments like these reaffirm the significance of the work I do with teams and organisations, helping their people develop skills that benefit them both professionally and personally.

Take action

Karl Weick was an organisational theorist who introduced the term 'sensemaking'.[69] This is a key capability for leaders and strategists alike, especially in VUCA times. Weick was referring to how we structure the unknown so as to be able to act on it.

Weick highlights the importance of taking action – even under uncertain conditions – with the story of soldiers lost in the Swiss Alps. Using a map found in an abandoned hut, they managed to navigate their way to safety, only later discovering the map was of the Pyrenees not the Alps.

This example highlights that movement, decisive action and close collaboration, even when they're based on imperfect information, can be critical in overcoming the paralysis that uncertainty often brings. Maybe the wrong map is better than no map, as in this example it proved useful as a tool to help the soldiers apply common sense and decisive action to get themselves to safety.

A PARABLE ABOUT UNCERTAINTY

A coaching client once shared an ancient Taoist parable that beautifully illustrates how uncertain outcomes often unfold in unexpected ways.[70] It's particularly helpful for people who, let's say, find it tough when things don't work out as they hoped or planned, ie when life throws them a curveball.

A farmer and his son had a horse who helped the family earn a living. One day, the horse ran away.

The neighbours exclaimed, 'Your horse has gone, what terrible luck!' to which the farmer replied, 'Maybe so, maybe not.'

A few days later, the animal returned home, leading some wild horses back to the farm. This time, the neighbours called out, 'Your horse has come back and brought several others with him. What great luck!' to which the farmer replied, 'Maybe so, maybe not.'

The following week, the farmer's son was trying to tame one of the wild horses and was thrown to the ground, breaking his leg. The neighbours called out to the farmer, 'Your son broke his leg, what terrible luck!' to which he replied, 'Maybe so, maybe not.'

The next month, soldiers marched through the town, recruiting boys for the army. They did not take the farmer's son because he had a broken leg.

The neighbours shouted, 'Your boy is spared, what tremendous luck!' to which the farmer replied, 'Maybe so, maybe not. We'll see.'

In complex environments, it's not just external uncertainty that challenges leaders. It's also the way our minds try to simplify and control what's happening.

Jennifer Garvey Berger's work on Mindtraps[71] offers a powerful way to understand five common mental habits that can unintentionally limit our leadership. These include the lure of simple stories, the comfort of being right, the pressure to agree, the drive for control and the pull of ego.

These patterns are natural and are often reinforced by traditional leadership cultures. For example, many leaders are rewarded for being in control, but in complexity, letting go of control can unlock greater clarity and collective intelligence.

Instead of asking, 'How do I stay in control?' try asking, 'How can I create the conditions for success, rather than control the outcome?'

Similarly, the need to be right can block deeper listening or new insight. Try asking, 'How might I be wrong?'

While agreement can feel comfortable, it's often dissent that sparks innovation. Try asking, 'How could disagreement help us here?'

Naming these mindtraps gives us more freedom to lead with intention. It creates space to be curious, adaptive and open, especially when the path forward isn't clear.

In complexity, better questions often matter more than perfect answers, and that's important to being a good strategist.

Actions

- **Practise tolerance**: Choose a day to consciously and intentionally notice and sit with a degree of discomfort caused by uncertainty, ambiguity or not knowing.

- **Uncertainty zone**: Identify a situation where you're waiting for more clarity and/or certainty. Start to take action regardless.

- **Reframe risk**: Identify a situation or decision with clear risks involved and ask yourself, 'What's the smallest action I could take to test this? What's a small "safe-to-fail" experiment?' Then act with clear intentions, experimenting in the micro.

- **Use the change curve**: Consider how this is currently playing out in your own life and work, and how you may have multiple curves all happening simultaneously and at different speeds in a non-linear fashion.

- **Control triggers**: Keep a journal of when you feel the need to control outcomes. Observe how you feel and what you think – and what ultimately happens over time.

Key takeaways

- Uncertainty is a constant in strategic environments. It reveals leadership character.

- Good strategists navigate ambiguity rather than avoid it. Strategic progress doesn't require full clarity – just direction and momentum.

- Perfectionism and control-seeking behaviours will hinder adaptability.

- Embracing experimentation builds resilience and agility; learning through iteration builds confidence.

- Decision paralysis often stems from fear of the unknown. Creating micro-strategies or 'placing small bets' supports decision making under uncertainty and encourages progress.

- Self-awareness and self-trust are powerful assets during times of uncertainty.

Remember Billie? Billie thrives on uncertainty and change. She recognises at all times where she is on the change curve and encourages her team to do the same. Good communication is always important to Billie, but she knows it is essential in times of uncertainty. She allows her team to see her vulnerable side, and as a result, however uncertain they may feel, they know they can trust her.

www.teammandarin.com/
resources/bemorestrategic

8

Be (More) Future-Focused, Be A Visionary

'Be bold! Be ambitious!' Easy to say, but for many people, hard to do (without a gentle nudge).

Facilitating so many workshops with so many thousands of wonderfully different people has taught me a thing or two about the various ways people approach problems. Among the many differences, I would argue that the majority – looking across all demographics, psychographics and geographics – are more naturally how thinkers, rather than what thinkers. An even smaller group are why thinkers – but I will put those people to one side for the moment.

What do I mean by how thinkers? When you present how thinkers with a problem or situation, their default setting is to look for solutions and (quick) fixes. This is good, this is useful. The world needs people who act this way.

Let's imagine someone who has spent the past twenty years working in an operational role or environment, predominantly focused on and rewarded for achieving short-term results. The majority of their typical working day is about reacting to issues and solving problems (most likely involving people). They fire-fight.

As a result, there's a high chance that they will have become extremely good at their job. This in turn will have influenced the way they think, act and operate – and quite possibly, what they believe and assume.

As far as they are concerned, this is what is required of them, and of those around them. Being a how thinker is their superpower. It is understandably valuable to an organisation.

Unfortunately, there are downsides – collectively and individually.

Collectively, in an environment dominated by how thinkers, those who focus on the bigger picture – the what and the why thinkers – can struggle to be heard. Operational urgency crowds out longer-term thinking; the culture is shaped by the way the how thinkers operate.

Individually, by typically thinking near-term, the how thinkers rarely see past the first barrier or hurdle. Instead, they lock on to it. This becomes their sole focus – it's where they put their energies. They tend to move from obstacle to obstacle, solving what's immediately in front of them, rather than stepping back to ask: 'What's really going on here? Where are we trying to go?'

This is what's sometimes referred to as now-forward thinking – in contrast to future-back thinking, which we will examine later in this chapter. Again, this isn't a flaw. The ability to act quickly and deliver short-term outcomes is valuable, but as a default lens, there are downsides.

Being a how thinker limits your aspirations as you struggle to see beyond that short-term barrier or hurdle and what is going to be required to overcome it. It defines your timeframes and what you see as priorities. It also draws in most of your energy and attention, and possibly, depending on their thinking style, that of those around you.

As a how thinker, you operate in a reactive mode and mindset the majority of the time. Everything is urgent. Everything is a priority. Everything competes for your attention. As the saying goes, your energy is drawn to the urgent, not the important.

People often draw the analogy of a swan swimming across a lake. On the surface of the water, the swan looks extremely graceful, gliding effortlessly, but if you pan down below the surface, you will see the swan's legs paddling furiously, desperately trying to maintain its graceful image.

Does this sound familiar? If it does, ask yourself – how sustainable is this? Is there a better way?

Interestingly, if I ask the how thinkers in a group how much they feel they achieved in the last year, despite how busy they believe they've been, and how tired they say they are, they often reply that they don't really feel that they've achieved much at all. Certainly nothing of any note.

What does 'being busy' really mean? Does it provide a greater sense of worth or purpose? Does it bring fulfilment? Are busy people just going through the motions, possibly masking a feeling of being overwhelmed, frustrated or stuck in a rut?

A few years ago, I was involved in helping four business leaders to form a potential partnership and collaborate more, to the benefit of not only their own organisations, but also their sector. I was due to moderate a meeting between these four what we might describe as typical alpha males.

Arriving a little late, I discovered all four of them standing up, pointing and gesticulating wildly, talking over each other. I let the discussion naturally ebb and flow, until it reached something of a conclusion.

Then, I asked, 'What are you actually trying to achieve together?'

Silence.

'What do you mean?' asked one of them finally.

'Well, I could hear you all talking about what you should and shouldn't do next, so I am curious to know what the desired outcome might be. What do you actually want to happen as a result by, say, the end of the year?'

'That's a good question!' one of them exclaimed, completely seriously (I wasn't sure at first).

It's quite natural for people to just dive in, but think back to all the meetings or conversations you've been part of which seemed pointless or even turned sour. Did anyone push to get clear on the shared outcome?

Working through the how is critical – of course it is – but you'll achieve a lot more, and far more effectively, if you first clarify the why and the what. It's not always easy to do either – but stick with it. With the why and the what clear, the how conversation is far more productive and your outcomes tend to be far more ambitious and challenging.

The power of vision

If it's really worked on and believed in, a vision – being clear on the what and the why before you get too far into the detail of the how – is a game changer for people, personally and professionally. Examples from the past and present day of those who have embraced the concept of a clear vision include equal rights activist Rosa Parks (in a less conventional sense), pioneering researcher Marie Curie, brilliant inventor Elon Musk (controversially so), fearless suffragette Emmeline Pankhurst and the first computer programmer, Ada Lovelace, who had rare foresight.

Despite the remarkable achievements of people who have developed a clear vision, many in organisations have a bad perception of it as rather cheesy slogans and marketing phrases plastered over office walls. To help people understand the importance of having a clear vision, I like to use the simple concept of getting from A to B. If Point A is now, Point B is your ultimate ambition or destination. Knowing your destination determines almost everything – including all the decisions you have to make between now and then. Even as your day unfolds and you're faced with various options and choices as to where to focus your time and energy, what tasks to do in what order, pause, map them out, and ask yourself which one will get you to B sooner, faster, more efficiently, more effectively? Often just seeing this visually lands the point.

John F Kennedy's famous 'We choose to go to the Moon' speech in 1962,[72] which sparked the Space Race, is a powerful example of why vision is important – and how that plays out over time. It was in this speech that JFK famously said two things that reflect the value and importance of having a clear vision.

The first – 'We choose to go to the Moon in this decade and do the other things not because they are easy, but because they are hard' – highlights the importance of being as bold and ambitious as possible. The second – 'That goal will serve to organise and measure the best of our energies and skills' – highlights the role a clear vision plays in helping to galvanise a group of people around a set of priorities.

For the record, the moon-shot goal – perhaps the most quoted part of JFK's rhetoric and the part I want to highlight here – was actually made in an earlier speech before Congress: 'I believe that this nation should commit itself to achieving the goal, before this decade is out, of landing a man on the Moon and returning him safely to the Earth.'[73]

Interestingly, the reaction to the vision was mixed among scientists and engineers. Many senior engineers quickly dismissed it as being impossible, in part because the essential technologies had yet to be invented. However, over time, those same sceptics came on board and later acknowledged the immense value of JFK's vision in mobilising talent, promoting national unity and driving unprecedented technological innovation. It was a statement of intent arguably unparalleled in modern history.

A good, clear, well-understood vision, ambition or statement of the ultimate goal or winning aspiration will inspire, motivate and energise people. It creates alignment and will help drive decisions and prioritisation.

Don't be a headless chicken

Have you ever been a part of a group or team in which you felt as if you were running around like a headless chicken? No clear sense of direction, goal or end game?

Over time, my observation of teams like this is that two things happen, beyond the inevitable boredom, frustration and disengagement. People start to look for the exit – if they don't just check out completely. More importantly, people suffer, potentially becoming burnt out or unwell.

How do we stop this happening? We provide clarity on that B – we ensure everyone is aligned on the outcome they are collectively working towards.

This is as applicable in our personal lives as it is in a professional setting. It is why many high performers, from fighter pilots to elite sportspeople, believe in the power and science of visioning practices and approaches.

EXERCISE: The wheel of life

Use a simple wheel of life framework to reflect holistically on your life today. Rate different categories – for example, career, health and vitality, personal growth, family, relationships, meaning and purpose – from 1–10, helping you to surface where things are thriving and where attention might be required.

Reflect on which areas stand out as needing work, and explore small, meaningful ways to close the gap. Consider people you know who might have something useful to offer, especially those you may not have considered before (eg an old friend, a neighbour, a relative, a member of a team or group you're associated with etc).

Being bold

How much time do you spend thinking about the long term – about the future? In most organisations, you can usually determine a planning style – even if it is unwritten or unspoken.

I've helped hundreds of teams and organisations define their Point B (their vision, their ambition, their winning aspiration, their ultimate goal – whatever you choose to call it). Regardless of the usual cynicism found in any group while doing this sort of work, I sense the energy levels in the room palpably rising and the excitement building as people work through their own limiting beliefs, even their fears, and start to really push the boundaries of what their future could be, what that might look and feel like. That's a powerful force.

However, how bold and ambitious are people really being? How often in work and in life are the vast majority of us encouraged to be bold and ambitious?

Let me come back to countering the headless chicken experience described above. Here's what often happens next.

Let's imagine I'm working with a leadership team on the co-creation of their five-year vision or ambition, exploring and ultimately defining their desired future state (Point B). As B emerges, the benefits of this clarity become apparent – better prioritisation, easier decision making, more alignment and understanding, greater engagement – which helps remove some of the remaining cynicism.

As we work to add meaning to B and define what this vision means in practice, someone often poses a challenge to their colleagues. If they don't, I will.

'Guys, this is great, really exciting and everything – but could we not achieve B sooner if we just focused all our attention on making it happen?'

Usually, after a stunned silence, the answer to that question is a resounding yes.

As an aside, this reiterates why it's so important to co-create and to involve as many different people, voices and opinions in these conversations as possible. Everyone then takes more ownership of the output.

In this example, the first draft of the five-year vision quickly becomes one of several objectives for the next year instead. Teams develop a sense of urgency – and what's really possible. When the majority of the people in the room spend their days in the here and now, being swans and fighting fires, this sort of work requires something of a mind shift – but it is hugely energising for them.

If you're looking to get much clearer on what the potential outcome is or needs to be for a particular situation (eg in setting goals or defining objectives), simply keep asking, 'To what end?' It also helps to draft goals and objectives in the past tense from the outset, ie from an imaginary point in time just after the outcome in question.

PRIORITY ONE

I have worked with many clients whose leadership team operated in silos, ie as individuals. Partway through a visioning and prioritisation exercise I was conducting with one global organisation, there were fifty priorities for the next three to five years, all 'equally important'.

A few hours later, after some long overdue discussions and gentle facilitative support, the team whittled their strategic priorities down to just a single Post-it. That in itself would have been quite an achievement, but it's what followed that really amazed me. Someone suggested that they could probably just do this, if they all pulled together, cleared their diaries and committed.

Less than six weeks later, the goal they set themselves was ticked off – and that particular business has never looked back.

Future-back

If you can bring your vision of the future to life for people, even the how thinkers shift into more of a what mindset. They will start thinking future-back rather than now-forward. This shift in mindset helps them to be bolder, more ambitious, more challenging and more willing to stretch themselves and each other.

With a clear Point B, people are far better able to prioritise – and do so far more ruthlessly. They start to say no, narrow their focus.

With what you're ultimately trying to achieve pinned down – even if it's not beautifully presented or articulated, or fully defined or understood yet – people tend to be in a far better position to identify not only what needs to start, and start immediately, but also what needs to stop. In a strategy development workshop I was facilitating in Scandinavia, as the vision of the business crystallised and the priorities become clear, the legal representative looked at me with a rather startled expression, apologised and left the room. I discovered later that he realised a current acquisition that was in play was no longer going to fit with the future aspirations of the business – and he left to cancel the transaction.

For you as an individual, having clarity about your desired professional or personal future state – your ultimate goal, your vision, your image of your future self, whatever you choose to call it – naturally helps you prioritise what really matters to you. It's also useful if you struggle to say no. With Point B clear, it becomes obvious what you need to say yes to, and how urgently, and what you need to push down the road or rule out completely.

CASTLES IN THE AIR

I coached a successful entrepreneur a few years ago and in one particular session, chose to use LEGO Serious Play (see Chapter 6) to unravel and envisage his real hopes, dreams and aspirations. Much to his own surprise, he built a representation of a castle in the middle of his future aspiration landscape.

Back then, he literally had to draw the curtains in case anyone saw what we were working on (I believe he was rather concerned by what his staff would think), but less than a year later, from a standing start, the power of that experience led to him making his aspirations become reality. He acquired that castle – and it remains a successful part of his business portfolio and personal passion many years later.

In a personal setting, as well as an organisational one, it's important to be open to a totally blank-slate approach, ie understand that the future may look nothing like the past. This is where the future-back approach really helps.

Alongside this, identifying and managing risks – and understanding your own risk appetite – is an important attribute of any strategist. Being strategic requires a degree of risk taking. How can it not? If you're working in a team, or with friends and family, it's important to understand how your individual risk appetites might vary – and why.

We'll explore our relationship to risk – and failure – in Chapter 9 when considering our decision-making styles. For now, it's important to recognise that to be more future-focused, to be more visionary, you will need to take a few – perhaps well considered, perhaps prudent – risks.

Being a futurist

Let's take a moment to get clear on the terminology of a futurist. When I first worked in this field, I found the language all rather baffling.

In simple terms, being a futurist relates to how far out into the future you look (sometimes referred to and separated into time horizons). The further you look out, the further along the timeline from today, the greater the degree of uncertainty, and the wider the range of issues that may potentially become impor- tant. This is sometimes called the cone of uncertainty.

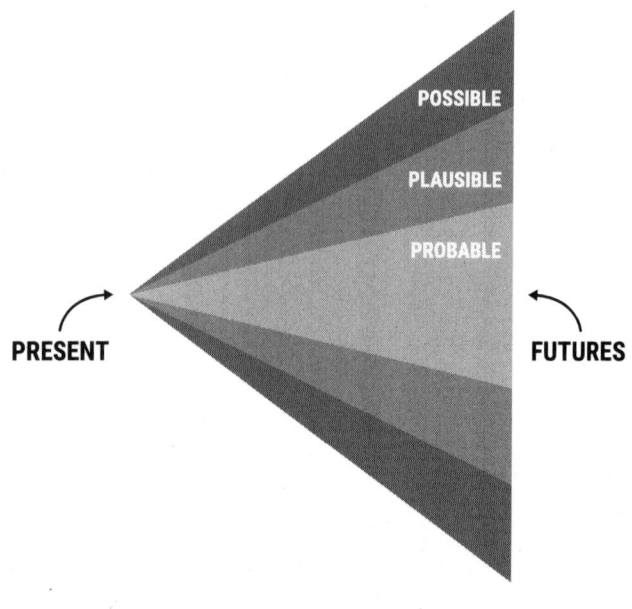

POSSIBLE

PLAUSIBLE

PROBABLE

PRESENT

FUTURES

Cone of uncertainty

Moving left to right along the cone, you or your organisation might develop scenarios, considering what's in vs outside your domain. For example, you work in the automotive industry and you're aware of a potential event or scenario in the future that is outside the scope of automotive, as it's perceived or defined today. This is where you may hear events or scenarios being described as black swans – low-probability/high-impact events inside your domain – or wild cards – unpredictable/high-impact events outside your domain. If you're serious about being a futurist, keep your eye on both!

In my early years of learning about foresight and strategy, I was told to avoid predictions. Instead of thinking about the future as something we can predict, we should imagine uncertainty rising and predictability falling – a kind of crossover. We then move from forecasting (what's right in front of us) to scenario planning (just out of sight), and eventually to dreaming or hoping (far out of sight).

When individuals set goals or create vision, you often hear phrases and expressions such as 'shoot for the stars' or 'reach for the sky'. I like to encourage my own children to reach over the houses – beyond the familiar, and towards something just out of sight.

In the same way we talk about Points A to B, we want to consider what's possible before we start to prioritise what's plausible – and finally, what's most probable.

Being future-focused

Too many people, teams and organisations base their picture of their future state on a projection of the present and the past – often drawing forward their existing biases, beliefs and assumptions. This is what we're looking to challenge – or at least be more aware of – as skilled futurists.

A classic example happens in businesses the world over. To set next year's targets, a manager simply looks at the targets from this year and extrapolates them forward. This might be satisfactory for twelve months – but any further out and they're probably missing something.

Choose your timeframe wisely. Don't just assume, for example, you need a five-year timeframe. If you have to consider multiple timeframes, go with the longest.

For example, if much of what you do is focused on the next six to twelve months, but you know there are certain aspects that will clearly require you to think further ahead – into at least years two and three – start with a three-year timeframe, if not longer. That's your B – your end point, your destination – and it will guide or frame much of your thinking.

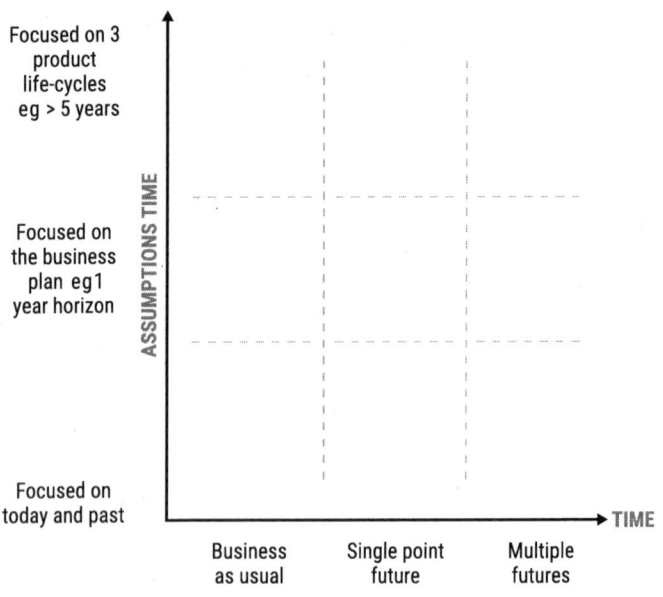

Timeframe vs future-focus chart

A client asked for my help in developing a longer-term strategy for his area of the organisation (circa 500 people). He later told me that his wife commented to him over the Christmas break that he seemed a lot more relaxed than she had ever seen him at that time of year. He realised that, for the first time in twenty years, he could benefit from some much-needed time off because his team was one year into a robust three-year strategy and delivery roadmap that every-body – himself included – understood and believed in. All he needed to do in the New Year was go back into work and continue rather than start all over again.

Having invited thousands of leaders to perform a simple strategic skills assessment over the years, I believe that being future-focused is an obvious blindspot for many. This isn't helped by a business world fixated on quarterly results and shareholder value. In fact, many leaders have blindspots about what's happening today – let alone what might happen in the future. (More on blindspots later.)

Being future-focused – and involving other people in the relevant conversations (ie co-creation) – is key to being a successful strategist.

Creating foresight

The strategy development process involves being forward-looking, working through options and making a clear set of interrelated choices about where you (or your team or organisation) are choosing to play or operate – and how you will win or succeed. This will require making decisions without all the information and with potentially high degrees of uncertainty. As Roger Martin puts it, 'True strategy is about placing bets and making hard choices. The objective is not to eliminate risk but to increase the odds of success.'[74]

With our strategy clear, we can start to plan. If we plan before our strategy is clear, we risk being caught out by black swan or wild card events. However, there's an important step missing in our development process before strategy.

It's the creation of foresight.

To think strategically and to develop robust future-proof strategy means being comfortable working with uncertainty (see previous chapter) as well as embracing external perspectives (the outside-in view). As change seemingly accelerates in an increasingly volatile interconnected world, leaders and their organisations are looking further and further ahead to better understand and foresee emerging opportunities and challenges.

There's no such thing as prediction. That's perhaps debatable now, given advances in AI, but I'll let the point stand as it's the next point that's more important here. The real value in foresight is opening doors to possibilities and opportunities. It's about exploring what *can* be, not what will be.

A useful tool

What tools might help you structure your longer-term thinking? The PESTEL framework has six categories – political, economic, societal, techno-logical, environmental and legal – which should be considered before making strategic decisions. The key here is, in the same way that we need to follow a cre-ation sequence of foresight then strategy then plan-ning, we must first gather insights about global shifts and future challenges *before* we make assumptions and draw conclusions about what is or isn't relevant (to us).

A tool such as PESTEL should help to ensure you have at least reduced the chances of having any blindspots. Now you need to prioritise what might matter most to you and your world over the next three to five years (choose your timeframe to suit). By assessing the potential implications of the most high-impact issues, trends and shifts, you will start to create those all-important insights. You will have fore-sight unique to you and your situation.

There are many benefits to considering alterna-tive futures, ie thinking about potential scenarios and mapping out Plans B, C, D and E. As we explored in the chapter on critical thinking, it makes it far easier to change course (from Plan A) as and when required, allowing you to be more agile and self-aware.

Start working regularly with futures and foresights, and your mindset will naturally shift. As a colleague once said to me, you move from 'information to affir-mation', meaning that you start to scan news and media differently, recognising trends and spotting patterns. You also realise that you know more than you first thought, and you have fewer surprises and potential blindspots as a result. This helps you to create patterns and spot emerging opportunities as well as potential threats and challenges. Get everyone in your team or organisation doing this and you're in a strong position.

While foresight informs longer-term decision making, there's a step you might want to take before that: looking backwards. This may sound counterintuitive, but to be more strategic, more future-focused, you need to use your rear-view mirror, to look backwards as well as forwards.

Of course, some things have changed in ways that were almost impossible to foresee – and incredibly fast too. Others changed rapidly for a period of time, and then seemingly stayed the same – think air travel over the last century. As William Gibson said, 'The future is already here – it's just not evenly distributed.'[75] Our task is to understand exactly what is changing, how fast and how significantly.

Project developer and writer Stewart Brand has done interesting work on the concepts of long-term thinking and layered time.[76] He also introduced 'pace layering', which illustrates and explores how different categories – and different components of civilisation – evolve at different speeds. As someone who's worked in almost thirty sectors, I find this particularly interesting, as even in a single day, I might shift focus from the energy sector to transport to retail – all operating within the same societal structures, but with their own speed of evolution.

Brand's pace layering image highlights how fashion and commerce have changed far faster than governance and culture.[77] In his illustration, Brand has these layers, in order of speed of change, from first to last:

- Fashion

- Commerce

- Infrastructure

- Governance

- Culture

- Nature

If we wind forwards a few years, this concept helps to explain why and how regulation has struggled to keep up with society's use of digital platforms and the flow and distribution of both information and value – but that's a different subject.

Horizon scanning

Now we can start looking ahead.

Strategists have their heads up – looking around them, today and into the future, gathering insights and perspectives from new, different sources. They scan wider and think broader, searching for potential signals and signposts – clues and indicators of what potentially lies ahead.

For example, a pioneering new technology is being trialled in sector x while being applied in sector y, albeit on the other side of the world. Is this a signal of what's to come? How else and where is this technology being applied? Meanwhile, country x is tabling a motion to change a regulation about y, while company a, which invests in country x, has made a surprising acquisition.

Strategists are curious and inquisitive, seemingly able to handle contradictory information. They always ask questions to better understand. Their ability to think both critically and creatively helps them to spot patterns and see connections, identifying potential opportunities as well as threats.

These activities are collectively referred to as horizon scanning, the practice of intelligence gathering of emerging trends, issues and uncertainties. As with any tool or technique, horizon scanning as an activity only becomes valuable when it creates insights that inform our decisions and our actions.

This is as true in a personal capacity as it is in a professional one.

Avoiding blindspots

One of the reasons why strategists horizon scan is to help us avoid blindspots. In the same way that we're taught to use our mirrors when we learn to drive, as strategists, we learn to spot unseen or unrecognised threats – or weaknesses – that have the potential to cause us harm now or in the future. In an organisational sense, this might simply be something that will undermine our success – or make being successful far harder, slower, more expensive or painful than it needs to be.

Importantly, strategists will spot not only their own potential blindspots – but also those of others. This has obvious benefits: you might see where your competitors have blindspots and exploit that situation; you might see blindspots that other members of your team, suppliers or partners have (which makes you increasingly valuable and important to them – assuming you share this insight).

Harvard Business School professor Michael Porter has warned that companies often continue to base strategy on outdated assumptions or industry norms – conventional wisdom that no longer holds true, yet still shapes decisions.[78] In my experience, business leaders are often made aware of potential blindspots, but for various reasons, they fail to act.

What might this mean in our personal lives? To answer this, I'll go back to a professional context.

I often ask people in strategy-related situations who they compete with. I ask the question straight up with no further explanation or guidance.

People nearly always answer this with 'Myself'. Occasionally, they say, 'My peers' – if they're being honest. A few say, 'Time'. The deeper thinkers might say, 'The future me' or 'My past self'. Quite profound!

However, it's rare – even for people in leadership roles who are exploring and defining their strategy – to respond that they are competing with an actual competitor to the business, ie a rival, another organisation that is stealing their customers and gaining share of the same market.

Maybe, just maybe, this reflects the lack of strategists in today's organisations – with so many naturally thinking inside-out rather than outside-in. To me, this comes back to how, for so many people, what they really need to do to achieve their goals – in life as well as business – is get out of their own way.

Balancing outside-in vs inside-out

Looking at your world inside-out means:

- Your beliefs, assumptions and behaviours are largely shaped by internal expertise and experience.

- You're often more connected to colleagues than customers, making it harder to see or understand what customers truly value vs what the organisation hopes they do.

- The organisation defines the market from its own perspective, which can make it harder to spot emerging opportunities or operate with real confidence in uncertain conditions.

Looking at your world outside-in means:

- You're viewing your organisation as customers and external experts might, bringing a fresh lens to long-held assumptions.

- You're identifying what customers may genuinely value, and spotting new or improved ways to deliver that value.

- Combining these external insights with your internal perspective, you create a more balanced and forward-looking view.

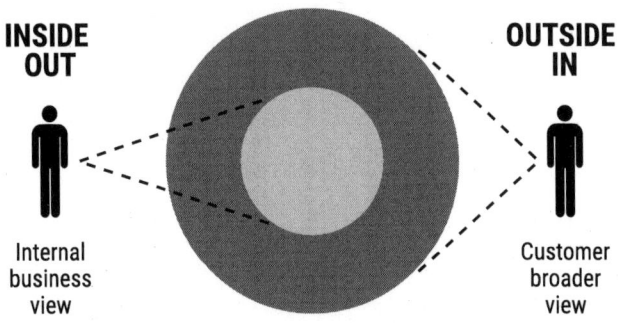

Inside-out vs outside-in perspective

When helping a team or organisation to create or refresh their strategy, I will normally start by considering a series of different lenses or perspectives – different positions and sources of insight that might help not only to inform what's possible, ie all the options (including scenarios, threats and opportunities) from which to make informed choices and decisions, but also to educate and probably jolt the team I'm working with, getting insights into the conversation that challenge people's existing assumptions and preconceptions. In a business setting, these lenses – and the respective insights – tend to fall into a few categories (depending on the nature of the work):

- **A set of inside-out insights** is what the team itself and other staff and stakeholders perceive, feel and believe to be true, for example the existing strengths, capabilities, weaknesses. If you've worked in a business context, you may have heard of PESTEL's little brother, the humble SWOT analysis. The SW is strengths and weaknesses – an internal view of a team or organisation – while the OT is opportunities and threats – an external view. It's important to handle these separately, but as an output to an exercise, it's remarkably useful.

- **A set of outside-in insights** from a variety of positions or standpoints, eg the customers – existing, loyal, lost, potential etc; the competition – however you wish to define it; the market or sector etc.

- Depending on the context, scope and aims, there might be a **time perspective** – looking at the past and the present.

- **Insights about the future** – or future-informed insight. This is where the creation of foresight comes in – which we explored earlier.

In a work setting, we might seek (or hide from) what's called 360-degree feedback from those we work for, those we work alongside, and those who work for us.

As a practitioner of the Leadership Circle Profile, I see first-hand the power of listening to 360-degree feedback and using this to create a powerful three-year development plan. We look for this feedback within our organisation – but also outside (eg customers, clients, partners and suppliers).

This kind of feedback is equally applicable in our personal lives. Who might have a potentially useful perspective on you, or on particular aspects of your life?

Being a visionary

We often think about the same people as being visionaries – and the same quotes – so I want to share a story about an arguably lesser-known visionary.

As a self-confessed space geek, I was tempted to use any number of well-known stories from our more recent history. However, I'm going a little further back in time to share the story of Robert Goddard, the father of American rocketry, who successfully launched the world's first liquid-fuelled rocket in 1926.[79] Nine years later, he achieved the first flight of a rocket with controllable direction. That's a big deal.

In late 1899, as a teenager inspired by HG Wells' science fiction novel *The War of the Worlds*, Robert climbed a cherry tree in his garden and looked up at the stars. He recalls being struck by an overwhelming desire to find a way to travel into space.

'I imagined how wonderful it would be to make some device which had even the possibility of ascending to Mars, and how it would look on a small scale, if sent up from the meadow at my feet.'[80]

He went on to say, 'I was a different boy when I descended the tree from when I ascended, for existence at last seemed very purposive.' This brilliantly captures his own emotional transformation.

Robert Goddard died in 1945, having only seen a few of the technologies he pioneered, but as the Space Race kicked in over the following two decades, many of his patents and innovations became crucial to the team at NASA.

I'll leave the last word to Robert Goddard, who quipped to his critics: 'Every vision is a joke until the first man accomplishes it. Once realised, it becomes commonplace.'[81]

Actions

- **Adopt a future-back narrative**: Dedicate time and energy to envisage and describe, in as much detail as possible, your life, or an important aspect of your life, five or more years from now. Better still, share this narrative with others and refine it through feedback. A popular exercise is called '**Future Headlines**', which involves creating the news headlines for that future date, in a world where your vision is now reality.

Reflect on how this feels and tap into the most positive motivations.

- **Trend scan**: Scan your horizons and choose one potentially high-impact shift or trend to explore in depth (using the guidance provided in this chapter). Block regular time, eg monthly, quarterly, to step back, zoom out and ask, 'What emerging trends and signals are on the edge of my awareness? What new threats and opportunities might appear?' Then zoom back in and ask, 'What does this mean for what I do next week or next quarter?'

- **Second-level thinking**: Most people stop at first-level thinking, the most immediate and obvious answer. Try asking yourself – and others – 'deeper' questions about the consequences of decisions, less likely outcomes and how others might respond.

- **Inverse planning (or back-casting)**: Instead of asking, 'What should we do next?' ask, 'If we had already achieved the long-term vision, what would have had to happen just before that? And before that?' This is back-casting, and it useful in strategy and coaching.

- **Scenarios thinking**: Explore multiple futures, not just the one you prefer. Map out at least three or four scenarios (eg status quo, optimistic, disruptive and wild card) and ask, 'What would I do today if this future were guaranteed?'

- **Reflect on risks and opportunities**: Reflect on a future vision, in work or in life, identifying what might potentially support or block your path to success. Use a simple two-column list. What matters most, and what action might you take to ensure progress?

Key takeaways

- Horizon scanning is only valuable when it leads to actionable insights that inform decisions and drive meaningful action.

- Anticipating the future is crucial in a fast-changing interconnected world, yet many organisations still focus only on short-term horizons.

- Effective strategists use foresight to spot opportunities, threats and blindspots, reducing reactivity and enabling proactive planning.

- Foresight is about exploring possibilities, not certainties, and relies on pattern recognition to imagine what could be, not just what is.

- Visionary leadership requires a bold future-back mindset, combining logic, emotion and narrative to craft compelling and believable visions.

Remember Billie? Billie embraces a future-back mind-set, continually scanning the horizons and acting on what she learns. She is aware of her blindspots and proactively counters them, helping her team to do the same. Her foresight is keen, based on her observations of the world around her.

www.teammandarin.com/
resources/bemorestrategic

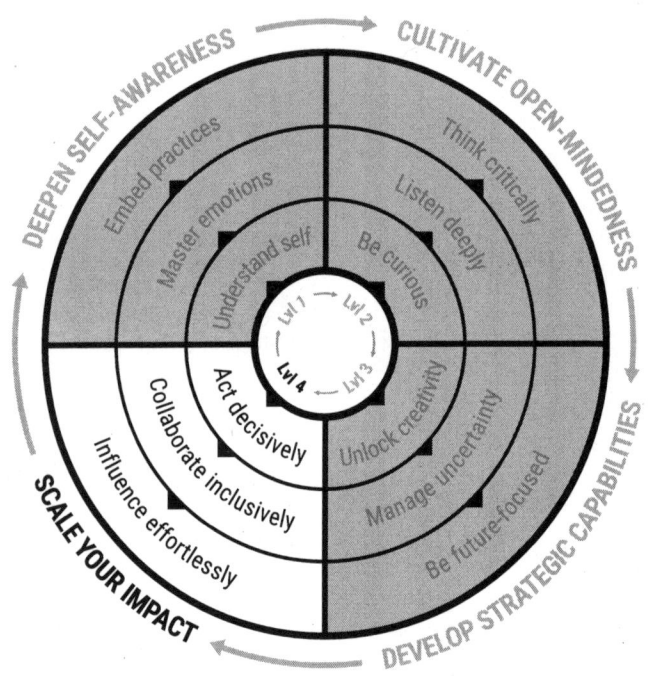

PART FOUR
LEVEL 4 PRACTICES – SCALE YOUR IMPACT

In Part Three – Develop Strategic Capabilities – we explored how to be comfortable with uncertainty and relinquish control, how to unlock our creative potential and be more whole-brained, and how to be visionary and future-focused. As you hone those skills, adopt the respective mindset and practise the related behaviours, you will certainly be more impactful – and that becomes more scalable and consistent with what we will explore in Part Four.

9

Be (More) Decisive, Be A Doer

Being (more) decisive is a valuable trait in any strategic leader – and more broadly, strategist – as it helps provide clarity and drive action and momentum. As a result, opportunities are more likely to be seized rather than lost.

Decisiveness is a learnable skill, despite what many people think. Preparation, of course, helps, as does clear accountability, confidence, experience and tuning into our instincts. Speed also plays an important role, ie being able to make decisions swiftly without sacrificing quality. Simplicity dictates how well we're able to do this.

Of course, it's important to consider the individual as well as the situation, as humans vary enormously in their decision-making style and approach. Let's consider an environment that requires particularly effective decision-making skills and abilities – floating around in space!

Neil Armstrong, who needs no introduction, was described by his fellow Apollo 11 crew member and astronaut Michael Collins as someone who 'makes decisions slowly and well … rolling them around his tongue like a fine wine and swallowing at the very last moment.'[82]

On the other hand, Frank Borman, who was selected alongside Collins as a member of the self-proclaimed 'Next Nine' (NASA's second selection of astronauts in September 1962) was described by Collins as 'aggressive, capable, makes decisions faster than anyone I have ever met … which would be even better if he slowed down a bit.'[83]

In this chapter, I will help you better understand your natural decision-making style (ie where you go when the stakes are high or when you're under pressure). To do this, we will explore your relationship with and perception of failure (your fear of making mistakes, or fears more generally) and how this influences your related behaviour. Making imperfect decisions is better than making none.

We touched on fears (and beliefs, limiting or otherwise) in Chapter 2 on self-awareness, and we explored the role of fear in how much we push ourselves to learn (vs staying comfortable) in Chapter 3 on learning. Fear is also linked to how much we overthink. Overthinking is often about circling around the consequences, and yet the best way to circuit break overthinking is action. That means making a decision.

FEEL-GOOD PROCRASTINATOR

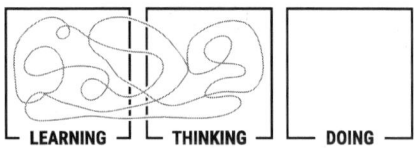

LEARNING   THINKING   DOING

SOMEONE MOVING FORWARD

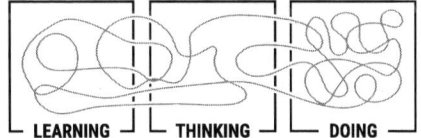

LEARNING   THINKING   DOING

Learning, thinking, doing: moving forward

Here, we will explore a set of tools and techniques to help you reframe failure – and learn to make faster, bolder and (hopefully) more positive decisions that align with your strategic priorities and longer-term goals and ambitions. Decision making, leadership and strategy go hand in hand in hand.

To have an impact on the world around us, yes, we need to be good at thinking – but also doing. We need to balance the time and energy we spend thinking through our options and clarifying our choices with making decisions. This means action, which means making progress and learning something new. Importantly, this includes choosing what not what to do, which Michael Porter called, 'the essence of strategy'.[84]

I have always liked this famous quote as it highlights the value of strategic decision making – and being able to clearly prioritise one thing over another.

233

In a business context, that's making conscious choices about investing and allocating the right resources in the right places for maximum impact (whatever that happens to be). It's also true in our personal lives – with the resources we're choosing to allocate being time, attention, energy, as much as our wealth and finances.

Our relationship with failure

To be the best, you need to make errors to improve and learn as quickly as possible. That's true for many people, even those in the public eye whom we view as highly successful at what they do. From James Dyson to Vera Wang to Reid Hoffman to Jeff Bezos – all of these individuals experienced some fairly monumental failures in their careers and working lives before achieving their more widely recognised successes.

The subject of failure, failing and learning from failure takes up a lot of column inches these days, so I won't attempt to compete with the experts here. However, I will comment on what this looks like in many of the teams and organisations that I've worked with over the years, and the cultures that they sometimes inadvertently create and promote.

Let's go back to looking at this from an individual perspective. Most of us still fear failure – to a greater or lesser degree – no matter how much coaching we receive, no matter how many courses we attend. I would wager a large bet that the vast majority of people don't take action, however significant or not, for fear of failing in one way or another.

The difference in attitude and mindset really stands out when I spend time with people from a high-performance background. They play to win, even in mundane everyday situations (which can be quite comical, when I'm simply setting up a workshop). However, in many teams and organisations that I've worked with, the fear of failing and the associated thoughts, feelings and behaviours are, perhaps inadvertently, encouraged through rarely challenged established routines and practices. Put another way, these thoughts, feelings and behaviours are being promoted through overt practices and cultures.

Ask yourself this: in your own working environment, are you rewarded for being right, or are you rewarded for taking action and learning as a result? Many people will say that they feel they need to be right, and many, depending on their background, believe they were taught to be right. People are often empowered to make a decision in their workplace because they are trusted to get it right. Therefore, if they get that decision wrong, they have failed. They have lost that trust.

At the same time, not many leaders, teams or organisations that I've experienced reprimand the choice *not* to make a decision. If someone delays or defers a decision, continuously waits or procrastinates – or possibly escalates the decision – that's OK. People are not reprimanded for doing nothing – or, as the expression goes, 'playing not to lose' – but these same people are reprimanded for getting it wrong.

For many, doing nothing – and losing an opportunity – feels safer than going for it and – potentially – getting it wrong. If this resonates, take a moment to think about where this need for safety originates – see Chapter 2 on self-awareness for more detail and guidance. Compare this to the high-performing teams and environments where playing to win dominates the culture. Notice the difference?

A learning culture

Increasing numbers of organisations work hard to adopt and develop a learning culture – one that emboldens people to think differently, to take risks and challenge the status quo, to continuously learn and take personal responsibility and ownership. Some standout exemplars of this in the business world include Microsoft, Google (Alphabet), Bridgewater Associates, Pixar and Adobe.

What do these companies have in common? They are arguably more adaptable, more agile, more resilient and more innovative than their contemporaries. They adopt a growth mindset – which we discussed in Chapter 3 – across the organisation.

That is why a learning culture – one that encourages risk and is comfortable with getting things wrong (some call this failure) – is increasingly integral to many organisations' strategy. You see the word 'learning' everywhere. One organisation I work with has reframed the word fail – it is now universally recognised as an acronym for First Attempt In Learning.

In this increasingly VUCA world, more and more teams are realising that they must embrace change and adopt a learning culture organisation-wide – or accept that they are effectively moving backwards.

As Mark Zuckerberg once said in a commencement address, 'The biggest risk is not taking any risk. In a world that is changing really quickly, the only strategy that is guaranteed to fail is not taking risks.'[85]

Decision-making types

What can you do to enhance your decisiveness? To become more decisive? That depends on not only your individual decision-making type or style, but also the context.

It's important to recognise the role of context in *all* our decisions. For example, the culture we operate in (workplace, social group etc) will affect the degree to which mistakes are accepted and learning is (genuinely) embraced – or not. Relationships with other people – from our parents to our partners to our customers and line managers – will be key to how we make decisions – or not.

However, exploring how we approach decisions, especially under stress, also helps us better understand our relationship with failure, ie how we (really) feel about failure – and failing. The eight dominant decision-making types set out below are about the individual – your motivations, thoughts, feelings and behaviours around decision making, especially when you are 100% accountable for that decision and the stakes are high. There will naturally be overlap between these types (there are usually patterns spanning the types and situations), so this is about identifying your dominant behaviours and underlying motivations.

EXERCISE: Learning from your past decisions

Before we look at the types, take a few moments to identify a significant decision from your recent past – one that made you feel more stressed, anxious or under pressure than normal. It's important that you were accountable for this decision, not simply being asked for an opinion by the decision owner.

Reflect on these questions:

- How do you feel when thinking about the decision?
- How did you feel when you made it (or chose not to make it)? Did these feelings help or hinder?
- What were you telling yourself, ie self-talk/ internal monologue?
- What delayed you and/or made it hard to make the decision?
- What might you learn from this reflection? What insights has this given you?

For each decision-making type, I've given advice for what those in that category might do to improve and enhance their decisiveness. Of course, this is not mutually exclusive – the advice for one type will most likely help another.

Which types resonate with you the most?

Perfectionist

You must be right, have to be perfect. Unfortunately, perfection is impossible, so you procrastinate.

Advice: Aim for speed rather than trying to predict the future. Reframe 'I don't fail' to 'Look how much I can learn'.

Analyser

You must have *all* the information before you make a decision. More validation, more robustness.

Advice: Remember that it won't be the 'right' decision forever. Even the best choices become outdated (faster now than ever). Use the 40/70 rule, adopted from the military – make a decision with less than 40% information, then you're shooting from the hip; wait until you have more than 70%, and you have waited too long.

Down-sider

You're overly focused on the risks of getting it wrong – or unable to balance these risks with the rewards of getting it right. If you're focused solely on the downside, it's hard to see what you lose with no decision. A variation on this type is the catastrophiser, who takes the decision personally and ruminates on the personal risk.

Advice: Re-evaluate the upside. What do you lose if you fail to make a decision? Think about the risk vs reward of making the decision *now* (or soon, at least). Force yourself to think through the negative side of *not* deciding. The downside of getting it wrong might be less than doing nothing (eg tying up resources unnecessarily). For the catastrophiser, ask yourself if you're imagining troubles. Can you control them? Think about Stephen Covey's circle of influence (Chapter 7).

Procrastinator

You will wait, delay, defer, not deciding (yet). You tend to hope the decision will be overtaken by events, but opportunities are lost and the delay potentially raises the stakes.

Advice: Ask yourself, is a more desirable option available right now? Can the decision be chunked down into smaller, less risky decisions? Give yourself a deadline.

Socialiser

You share the decision, and ownership, with others. Are you consensus-gathering, making it a decision by committee? Are you passing the buck?

Advice: Ask yourself why you're not fully owning the decision. Show leadership, trust your gut instinct and believe in yourself.

Complexifier

You make the decision unnecessarily complex (or even impossible).

Advice: Aim to simplify. Reframe the decision. Chunk it down.

Democrat

You make the most popular choice, hiding behind the optics. You know the right thing to do, but it's hard for you to do it if others don't like it.

Advice: Be respected, even if not popular. This is a test of character. Live by your values – or the values of the team or organisation.

Maverick

You decide and act quickly, then think later. Perhaps you are too eager to find out what happens next.

Advice: Check your motivations. Are you avoiding blame or loss of pride or ego? Let's pick up on a few key points that span multiple types and styles.

Key strategies

Be clear on the outcome or goal

With absolute clarity about the destination, your choices become infinitely easier. This goes back to the simple A to B concept. I find this is particularly true in day-to-day life. If someone is really clear on what they ultimately want in life – or what they want to achieve this year, week or day – they tend to be much more able to push past options that are only going to distract them and act on opportunities that will accelerate their progress.

Put a clock on the decision

Time-capping really helps. Be clear on the deadline. If a decision is to be made by Friday afternoon, ensure the necessary work has been done *before* Friday afternoon so that the best possible decision can be taken at that time.

Simplify

Chunk down. Identify options and break larger, more complex decisions into more manageable parts to ensure progress. Can you make the decision even more straightforward? (See decision-making tools below.)

Learn to trust your gut

For our perfectionists and analysers, and those with any sense of self-doubt, remember that you've been trusted with the authority you have to decide for a reason. Your experience, your skills, your knowledge and your beliefs (and, no doubt, your potential) have all contributed to that being the case, and your gut feel is the sum of those. Learn to get comfortable with authority and accept that, at times, you will need to swim against the tide and feel the fear. Read the Chapter 3 section on stepping out of the comfort zone into the learning zone.

Decision-making tools

There are many decision-making tools you can learn to use, but you can save a lot of time and get close to the same result by creating your own ranking or assessment tool that suits your particular context, style or situation.

It's important that you're able to compare potentially incomparable options. For example, Billie needs to decide where best to allocate her team's limited resources, time or effort. To do so, she must choose between a series of options. Does she focus all in on a new marketing and advertising approach, possibly a re-brand, or on PR/influencing? Does she prioritise funding a new factory and explore a potential joint venture with a supply chain partner?

As Reid Hoffman advocates in *Harvard Business Review*,[86] simply dividing the options into low, medium, high priority might suffice to make Billie's decision clear. Alternatively, here are some concepts or approaches, some of them similar to the 40/70 rule described above, that might be useful, depending on the situation.

The 80/20 rule

Also called the Pareto Principle, this is about focusing on the activities and decisions that will have the greatest impact on the desired outcomes.[87] Again, this works in life as much as it does in business.

Try this: look at your diary for the last three days and list every single activity you've been involved in. Now categorise these by the value they provided in terms of how much they contributed towards you achieving one of your main goals for the next six to twelve months. A simple low, medium, high grading will work, as will grading them one to five (one being the lowest, five being the highest).

Rewrite that list of activities in the order they add value to you achieving your goals. Now look ahead at the next three days. Is there anything in your diary you need to add, remove or reprioritise?

The 10-10-10 rule

This simple method is designed to help you evaluate a decision's potential impact over three timeframes – ten minutes, ten months and ten years. It ensures that you're taking both short- and long-term consequences into consideration, ultimately leading to more informed choices. This is particularly good for life choices, and for situations that make you feel anxious or uncomfortable.

Try this: identify a decision you're currently weighing up, either in life or at work. First, consider how you will feel immediately after making that decision – and for the next ten minutes. Then, evaluate the potential impacts of that decision on all aspects of your life and work over the next ten months – and how you feel about those. Finally, imagine the long-term implications of that decision and how it might shape your life and work over a ten-year timeframe. Again, how will you feel about those?

70/90 Rule

Jeff Bezos, Amazon's High Lord, believes some decisions are 90% decisions, ie they require you to have 90% of the relevant information before making them.[88] You need to recognise how much more time and resource intensive these decisions will be to make. Most people decide that 70% of the relevant data is actually enough.

Bezos also talks about decisions being either one-way or two-way – as in doors. One-way decisions are irreversible, so they are naturally more significant as the consequences are permanent. These decisions demand the most time, resources and attention.

Two-way decisions are reversible – you can walk through the metaphorical decision door, and then come back again. These decisions require far fewer resources – and should be made far faster.

OODA Loop

The decision superiority model, also known as the OODA Loop, is widely applied in businesses and governments the world over, but its origins trace back to the Korean War, when Colonel John Boyd studied why the USA's inferior fighter jets were so superior in terms of aerial combat effectiveness (or kill ratio). Boyd, a renowned fighter pilot and later US Air Force Colonel, was dubbed forty-second Boyd for his standing bet as an instructor pilot: 'From a position of disadvantage, he will defeat any opposing pilot in a dog-fight in less than forty seconds.'[89]

How? In one word, tempo.

Boyd realised that the superior training of the USAF pilots allowed them to make rapid decisions, and that negated the inferiority of their aircraft. He codified his theories into what is known as the Observe, Orient, Decide, Act (OODA) Loop.

How does a fighter pilot – or anyone – use this in practice?

- **Observe**: what is happening, what data is coming in? What do you see, hear, read, feel?

- **Orient**: how does this relate to your current situation? What changes? What do you want, what are your goals and risks?

- **Decide**: what are your options? Choose one.

- **Act**: execute. Boldly and confidently implement your decision.

The outcome? A disruption of the flight path that would normally be expected. It's unpredictable and asymmetrical – resulting in confusion of the enemy. The really clever bit? The cycle is repeatable.

If a series of manoeuvres can be accomplished with such speed that the adversary cannot react with appropriate counter-manoeuvres, then victory is certain. Boyd's insights into rapid decision making have influenced military strategy and tactics – and posthumously, he became known as the 'original Top Gun'.

Ask yourself: what's your decision-making tempo? How often do you need to refresh? How long does it take – or how long do you need to wait to look for results (and learn)? How might you speed your own cycle up – or potentially slow down that of your competition or your adversaries?

Approach vs avoidance

Would you prefer to aim to win or to seek not to lose?

Goals can be classified as approach goals or avoidance goals, based on whether you are motivated by wanting to achieve a positive outcome (eg I want to succeed at this project) or avoid an adverse one (eg I don't want to fail at this project).

Psychological studies in goal-setting theory and motivation suggest that creating approach goals, or positively reframing avoidance goals, is beneficial for wellbeing, more sustained motivation and better performance.[90] Conversely, when you're dreading a tough task and expect it to be difficult and unpleasant, you may unconsciously set goals around what you don't want to happen – avoidance goals – rather than what you do want. This can lead to anxiety, rumination and reduced satisfaction.

Playing to win is empowering. It's rooted in the belief that you *can* win and gives you a fighting chance to rise to the occasion. When you play to win, you understand you don't have to be perfect; you just have to do your job – take note, perfectionists and analysers!

This is like pulling the trigger on a decision: once you've committed, especially with a play to win mindset, you tend to act more decisively. Familiarity with the task or situation helps lower the perceived threat, which calms your fears and quietens activity in the amygdala (your brain's alarm system). With fear dialled down, you can perform more confidentially, play more fearlessly and become more motivated or enticed by the rewards ahead.

Playing not to lose, on the other hand, reflects a preventive mindset – one that activates your sense of fear and risk aversion. When you're focused on avoiding negative outcomes rather than pursuing positive ones, your thinking becomes more defensive, even destructive. This is the mental equivalent of sitting on a decision. Instead of thinking, 'I hope I make this shot', you're more likely to think, 'I hope I don't miss'. The difference may seem subtle, but it's powerful because now 'missing' is the dominant thought.

Here's the simple neuroscience: the most prominent thought in your mind is the one your brain is most likely to act on (and most likely to occur). If you're thinking about how much you don't want to lose, losing becomes the focus. If you're thinking about how much you want to win, winning is the prominent thought. Your actions tend to follow your dominant thoughts, often unconsciously.

I ask again: would you prefer to aim to win or to seek not to lose?

A successful decision isn't about finding the perfect option. For business leaders, for example, it's often better simply to choose a path and start walking down it rather than getting stuck in endless analysis and debate. How many of you have had a meeting about a meeting simply because someone – including yourself – failed to make a decision?

Ellen Langer, a professor of psychology at Harvard University and a pioneer in the field of mindfulness, has long emphasised that it's more important to make decisions work than to obsess over making the perfect decision.[91] She argues that this perspective encourages individuals to bring awareness, flexibility, commitment and presence to their choices, making the choices right through how they respond and adapt, rather than being paralysed by the need for certainty and waiting for the 'right' choice to appear.

Back to Jeff Bezos, whose multiple soundbites on decision making underscore a similar philosophy: 'decide and commit'. While thoughtful decision making is valuable, over-emphasis on the right choice can leave us feeling stuck. What truly matters is how we commit to making any choice successful.

This approach works for two reasons:

1. **Decisions aren't destiny**: No choice guarantees success, and no single decision dooms us to failure. Outcomes are shaped by the effort, creativity and persistence we bring after deciding. Whether it's a decision on a career change, a project goal or personal priorities, what happens next makes the difference. Once you've chosen, go all in. It's this effort that transforms a good decision into a great outcome.

2. **Action beats analysis**: Spending too much time weighing every detail can lead to paralysis by analysis. Often, there's no clear right choice, just a set of possibilities. Decide with the best information you have, trust your intuition and commit to moving forward. Which decisions are you potentially overthinking? How can you shift your focus from finding the perfect path to creating success with the path you choose?

Identify your best choice and commit to making it work – and take action.

Actions

- **Reflect on failure**: Journal or talk through a time when a specific decision you were involved in led to an unexpected learning.

- **Decision log**: Create a simple log to track your choices – in work and in life – and their learning outcomes.

- **Bias for action**: Notice when you're unsure about a choice or decision, and intentionally choose doing over waiting.

- **Adopt tools**: Experiment with the various tools provided in this chapter (eg decide with less than 70% of the information).

- **Assess your decision-making style**: Look at this in different situations and reflect on the advice given in this chapter.

- **Empower your team**: If you lead or manage others, do you reward the person who admits their mistakes and shares what they learned? Do you discourage non-decisions? How are you going to reward the required behaviours in others?

Key takeaways

- Execution makes strategy real. No decision, no traction. Strategic action involves a degree of calculated risk.

- Progress beats perfection – especially early on in a process. Action builds confidence and opportunities to learn (learning loops).

- Failure aversion delays decisions and progress. Not deciding is a decision that has its own consequences.

- Decision making can be structured and agile. Decisiveness is a muscle built by action and experience, not contemplation.

- Start small, scale fast – this is how bold ideas grow.

Remember Billie? As someone who is as well respected and liked in her personal life as she is in business, Billie knows the importance of owning her decisions. She will never allow an opportunity to pass her by simply because it may not be the right decision. Knowing that any decision is better than no decision, she and her team have built a culture in which failure is celebrated as a learning opportunity. Everyone recognises their decision-making style and arms themselves with the tools and techniques to counter or complement it.

Once they have agreed on a decision, they all commit to making it work. As a result, Billie and her team are agile, responding rapidly to the changes they see around them and staying a few steps ahead of the competition.

www.teammandarin.com/
resources/bemorestrategic

10
Be (More) Inclusive, Be A Collaborator

In an increasingly uncertain hyper-connected world, complex problems require diverse perspectives and collective expertise. Truly effective collaboration, though difficult, helps create engagement and alignment towards a common goal, accelerating innovation and progress, and making previously insurmountable targets seem within reach. Being collaborative means harnessing collective intelligence for strategic impact – benefitting from the wisdom of the crowd. [92]

The co-creation drum will be banged hard throughout this chapter because strategy is not something you do on your own. As consultant and researcher Max McKeown wrote, 'Strategy is not a solo sport, even if you're the CEO.'[93]

I have facilitated many workshops for the Future Agenda programme, which works with experts all over the world. The sessions showed how important it is to co-create – to have diversity in your teams, insights and perspectives – and how important it is to play, be imaginative. You need the right environment for that to happen naturally and comfortably for everyone (psychological safety, as outlined in Chapter 6).

Good strategists seek challenge as much as they do insight and learning. They actively look to co-create and to be more inclusive, recognising and appreciating diverse perspectives and fostering an environment where everyone has equal opportunities to – and feels safe to – contribute and challenge. Strategists tend to be the people who walk into a meeting room or event space and sit next to a complete stranger rather than sidle up to their friend or colleague. They are the people who proactively choose to change seats in a workshop (it's amazing how many people own their space in a room).

Good strategists have developed the skills, awareness and discipline to leave their pride, fears and ego at the door of any strategic conversation. They recognise that true collaboration is fundamental to higher-level thinking – from problem solving to visioning to execution. They know that real, sustainable impact is not achievable on their own and that being able to collaborate well is far more than a strength – it's a superpower. It is a strategic necessity in work and in life.

The good news is having read so far, you have all the skills you need.

What is collaboration?

Collaboration is the process of people working together towards a shared outcome, pooling resources and skills as necessary. It requires open communication, mutual respect and shared responsibility among all participants.

The most diverse collaborations are often the most successful. We have seen in earlier chapters how we benefit from the broadest possible set of perspectives. Studies back this up, concluding that more diverse groups benefit in terms of creativity, productivity and problem solving.

A 2023 McKinsey study showed a strong correlation between the gender and ethnic diversity of executive teams and business performance.[94] The teams with both types of diversity are on average 9% more likely to outperform their peers.

Another study showed how teams diverse in gender, age and geographic location made better decisions up to 87% of the time – putting the bias of groupthink to bed.[95] We'll explore that particular bias later in this chapter.

However, diversity isn't without its challenges: miscommunication, misalignment and misunderstanding, including cultural. Working with many global teams, I know this is often the area that requires the most time and attention.

In fact, throughout history, there are examples of cultural misalignments happening, often due to race, class or other barriers. For example, Benjamin Banneker (1731–1806) was a brilliant astronomer, mathematician and surveyor who helped design Washington DC – but because of his race, he was often excluded by the scientific community at the time. Dr Chien-Shiung Wu (1912–1997) was a key figure in nuclear physics who helped disprove the law of parity, a breakthrough that won her male colleagues the Nobel Prize in 1957. However, she was excluded.

Collaboration is purposeful

Collaboration is deliberate. It is not about consensus for consensus's sake.

Carefully considered design and structure of meetings and workshops, as well as skilled facilitation, helps ensure the right people are being engaged for the right reasons. Everyone must be clear on their reason for involvement at what stage – and what their particular role is at any time.

In fact, clarity of roles in collaborative efforts reaps great rewards in terms of their strategic impact – with everyone pulling in the same direction. For example, the Apollo programme, which culminated in the 1969 Moon landing, involved over 400,000 engineers, scientists and support personnel working across numerous organisations to achieve this historic goal.[96]

No doubt, many of you spend a lot of time in meetings. 'Too many meetings' is a phrase I hear every week. Take a moment to think about two or three meetings you've attended recently, for work or in your life. Can you remember who was there? Do you know why they were there? What was their role? How were they contributing towards the outcome? Was the outcome itself actually clear? If you asked them, would they know why *you* were there?

How well was the meeting structured? How well were your collaboration efforts channelled towards achieving the outcome? What worked well? What might you do differently next time? What might you try, ask or suggest?

A purposeful meeting is a better meeting.

Collaboration is a superpower

Collaboration is sometimes seen as being a weakness, ie a team or individual is perceived to be unable to achieve something on their own – so they have to seek help. I disagree. Being able to collaborate effectively is an incredible strength – even a superpower.

Most teams I meet are average in terms of performance and compared to some of the best I've encountered. Only to start with, of course. (If I've worked with you – no offence; I meant someone else!)

Very few teams genuinely collaborate, even though many say that they do. In my experience, as awareness rises and more people share their views and challenges, there's nearly always an acceptance that yes, maybe they're not quite as collaborative as they first thought.

What's happening? Ultimately, the people in the team don't fully trust each other. Post Covid, many don't even really know each other – so how could they possibly trust each other? As the saying goes, 'with trust anything is possible; without trust, nothing is possible.'

Spend a prolonged period of time with just one truly high-performing team and you will see and feel what true collaboration is. The trust is palpable, and trust is a precursor to any effective teamwork (see the importance of trust section coming up). Psychological safety, as introduced in Chapter 6, is also vital. Every member of a high-performing team, no matter their role or position, feels safe to share ideas, ask (any) questions and challenge each other without fear of judgement or repercussion. There is no blame. People are accountable. They don't walk past problems.

A two-time Olympic gold medallist who I work with in the business world often reminds me of what real collaboration – and teamwork – looks and feels like. 'Remember, Charlie,' he says, 'good teams ask for help, great teams offer it.'

He's right, of course. His pertinent point is what he's saying about great teams, but what is he saying about good teams compared with the average ones?

I have worked in and alongside hundreds of teams and it's rare that I witness anyone genuinely feeling comfortable enough to ask for help, at any time, from anyone. It's certainly a hard team environment to foster – but it's a powerful one.

THE RISE OF CO-PETITION

A handful of leaders are brave enough to get into bed with their enemy, sometimes for the benefit of the greater good, but usually for mutual benefit. The trend is on the rise, especially in industries facing rapid technological advancements and high research and design costs, as the collaborators are able to pool resources, sharing the costs and the risks.

This means that a traditional competitor may become a potential customer – and loyal customers may become potential competitors, all at the same time. This certainly requires a different, more strategic way of thinking.

Famous examples include:

- Sony and Samsung forming a joint venture in 2004 to develop and manufacture flat-screen LCD panels.
- BMW partnering with Toyota to co-develop fuel cell technology.
- Microsoft developing software for Apple's platforms, with both benefitting by reaching broader audiences.
- Airbus and Boeing collaborating on safety and regulatory standards to ensure industry-wide efficiency.

There are also examples of collaboration between players in different markets, usually for innovation reasons, that sometimes surprise people. For example, Google and Levi's collaborated to create smart clothing, and AMEX collaborated with fashion brand Luar, helping the latter secure funding while the former gained access to a new market.

Why collaboration is so hard

Being collaborative is extremely hard to do well. Much of that comes down to human behaviour – including your own.

Take a moment to think back to the strategic mastery framework in Chapter 1, which underpins everything required to be a world-class strategist. Let's start with Level 1, the foundation practices required to build self-awareness and become more conscious of ourselves. I'll share a story to help make the connection.

As a leadership coach, I work with a model developed and tested over more than two decades by the brilliant Richard Barrett,[97] inspired by Abraham Maslow's Hierarchy of Needs (as explored in Chapter 2). The model identifies the seven areas that comprise human motivations – seven levels of consciousness, from basic survival to serving future generations. It acts as a map for understanding the values of those around you (your leaders, teams and other stakeholders), a powerful tool for developing more productive, purposeful relationships between them – right across an organisation.

Leaders grow and develop by learning to master the seven levels of personal consciousness (the leadership focus areas – or motivational levels – in the table) and seven levels of organisational consciousness.

The table also shows example themes for each level (key attributes or activities connected to that level) and example leadership roles (a practical leadership archetype tied to each level).

When I use this model with leaders and their teams, it's common for them to start a session proudly claiming to be collaborative – which is right up at

The seven levels of personal/organisational consciousness

Level	Focus Area	Human Motivation/ Organisational Consciousness	Example Themes	Example Leadership Role
1.	Viability/Survival	Basic needs, security, stability	Physical safety, crisis management	Crisis Manager
2.	Relationships	Connection, belonging, teamwork	Trust, communication, collaboration	Relationship Builder
3.	Performance/ Self-Esteem	Recognition, achievement, respect	Confidence, accountability, status, results	Performance Manager
4.	Evolution/ Transformation	Learning, change, innovation	Adaptability, continuous improvement	Facilitator/Influencer
5.	Alignment/ Internal Cohesion	Alignment with values, integrity, purpose	Ethics, culture, shared vision	Authentic Leader
6.	Collaboration/ Making a Difference	Service, contribution to others	Social responsibility, community impact, partnership	Mentor/Partner
7.	Contribution/ Legacy/Future Orientation	Sustainability, future generations	Long-term impact, stewardship, visionary leadership	Visionary

level 6 – before realising that this is perhaps inconsistent and lacking strong foundations. There is work
to do at some of the lower levels of consciousness –
personally and organisationally – to realise their collaborative potential.

Now let's explore Level 2 of the strategic mastery
framework – cultivating open-mindedness. What gets
in the way of this as we look to collaborate? It's those
pesky beliefs and fears, the less helpful thoughts and
the poorly timed emotional responses again!

Imagine the scene: you're in a conversation with
a brilliant potential collaborator and partner. If you
join forces, magical things could happen, but this person behaves in a way that sometimes gets under your
skin. They trigger you.

You have two options. You allow your emotions
to run the show (eg become defensive, appear frustrated, go silent) and possibly respond from below
the water line of the human iceberg (ie a position
of judgement). Alternatively, you tap into your
self-awareness practices from Level 1, choosing to
pause, breathe, consciously stepping up onto the balcony and thinking from a place of curiosity.

'That's interesting,' you say.

The skill of being genuinely able to listen to
understand and think coolly and calmly, even when
you vehemently disagree with another person's perspective, and continue the conversation to a mutually beneficial outcome takes great discipline, but
it is time well invested. Active listening exercises

really help to foster trust and collaboration between people.

For example, I've facilitated fishbowl discussions where one group of people converses while their colleagues observe and listen – often in a circle around the outside. It may sound strange, but it's remarkably effective. Similarly, I've facilitated group coaching conversations, in which people are only able to use a selection of classic coaching responses to encourage more listening and a move away from conversations being simply taking turns to talk. It's along the lines of the building your listening muscle exercise at the end of Chapter 4.

Better still, although this needs to be handled with great care, I've facilitated three-way coaching and feedback discussions, in which two people talk about the third, who is standing right next to them.

ALIGNMENT – OR NOT

Partway through a leadership team workshop, I asked if we could perform a simple check-in to see how aligned everyone was at that stage. I suggested that – given the focus of the session – the participants all take a few moments to capture and share their understanding of the new direction they were agreeing to take, ie what they had just decided.

'There's no need, Charlie – we're all aligned,' said the boss.

'Er, OK – then this won't take long,' I replied.

I asked everyone to write down their responses to a few simple questions based on what we had been exploring together for the past day or so. The first volunteer reported back – and the room went silent. The next person stood up, looking rather nervous, and said, quite literally, the polar opposite to the first person.

'Ah!' There were many lightbulb moments for that group that day – but one was quite simply how poor they were at really listening to each other. Everything else built from there.

Avoiding groupthink

For clarity, groupthink is not a good thing. It's a significant risk, not a positive dynamic such as brainstorming. It occurs when the desire for harmony or conformity within a team overrides critical thinking and open, honest debate. It's a major problem in teams and leads to suboptimal decision making, as history demonstrates.

Just look at the US Government's flawed decision making during the Bay of Pigs fiasco in 1961, or NASA's organisational culture issues preceding the Challenger disaster in 1986. These cases illustrate how groupthink can stifle dissent and result in catastrophic outcomes, underscoring the need for diverse perspectives and constructive challenge within any team environment.

Strategists encourage inclusion and a diverse range of perspectives. They know not to develop strategies in isolation and will actively pursue a collaborative approach, inviting new sources of insight and expertise. Open to new thinking, they challenge current assumptions and engage in discussions that are outside their traditional [business] comfort zone. They don't groupthink, they co-create.

Co-creation involves engaging and involving internal and external participants – customers, partners, employees or other stakeholders – to generate ideas, solve problems and enhance innovation. LEGO Ideas and Nike By You are two famous examples of this happening at scale.

In a recent workshop, one participant was clearly feeling threatened. He considered that I was suggesting others in the team might get involved in 'his' strategy and stated that he was the only one with the qualifications to work on the strategy for the organisation. Everyone else should stick to their respective roles and fields.

It's fair to say we disagreed.

We must work hard to eliminate groupthink and reap the benefits of co-creation and more inclusive environments. If you're working in any sort of team or group, if the context suits, find ways to hear from everyone – rather than diving into discussion and being pulled towards the louder voices or the most obvious or appealing ideas.

Ask everyone involved to capture their own thoughts, ideas, preferences etc on a card or sticky note. When everyone is ready and has written something down, invite them to turn their cards over, revealing their answers. Find a suitable way to process the outputs and proceed from there.

Tools such as Dr Edward de Bono's Six Thinking Hats,[98] in which people (metaphorically) assign thinking hats to help encourage and structure diverse perspectives, really help.

EXERCISE: Six thinking hats

This is a simple structured technique that is particularly useful when a group of people needs to evaluate a problem, idea or decision from a number of different perspectives – especially when they're trying to avoid the normal or obvious responses.

Most people have a preferred or habitual thinking style and apply this to *all* problems. This exercise helps them to step out of their normal box and discipline their thinking.

The hats each represent a thinking style. They are:

- White: likes facts – neutral, dispassionate, objective.
- Yellow: positive/constructive. Moves from dreams to logic, opportunity, making things happen.
- Red: emotions. This thinker makes their feelings known, uses hunches or intuition/gut feeling.
- Green: creativity – what's the alternative? This thinker is provocative, but doesn't shoot ideas down. Instead, they build and move on.

- Blue: takes a helicopter overview – what are we doing now? This thinker uses process to run things, watches to see who is contributing.
- Black: negative and gloomy, this thinker focuses on why something won't work.

There are many ways to use the technique – for example, share out the hats around the group, simply telling people their hat colour. Give each individual two to three minutes to adjust to their hat and generate a few initial thoughts, views, concerns or ideas, before launching into a group discussion (eg a brainstorm) with everyone still wearing their hats.

After five to ten minutes, swap the hats around – and repeat. For completeness, ensure each hat is worn by each individual, rotating through the hat colours. This works just as well – if not better – with pairs or groups wearing the same hat for a period of time before rotating.

If you know that you have a particularly creative or optimistic person in the group – or a particularly pessimistic person – invite them to evaluate a problem, idea or recommendation wearing the most diametrically opposed hat colour. The more fun you have with this, the better the outputs.

Let's now revisit Level 3 of the strategic mastery framework – being creative, comfortable with uncertainty and future-focused. These all benefit from involving other people and being collaborative.

What gets in the way? Fear of judgement? Limiting beliefs? Biases? Emotions and behaviour? All of the above?

In exploring how to be more creative in Chapter 6, I introduced the famous pasta tower game. Do you remember who won? The children. Why? Because they play together – they collaborate.

There's a reason I use so much LEGO Serious Play in my work.

The importance of trust

We accept that we need to be more inclusive of more diverse perspectives more often, but how do we put this into practice? In many ways, this brings us to Level 4 of the strategic mastery framework – achieving real, sustainable impact, directly and indirectly.

A strategist will use a combination of tools and techniques, frameworks and technology to channel their collaboration efforts into tangible outcomes, striving to make a genuinely useful impact. Depending on the context and the type of work, there's a whole range of tools and frameworks that you might choose from. Design thinking is one well-known approach that very much draws on the benefits of co-creation and iterative problem solving.[99]

I'm sure many of you have been involved in brainstorming activities – so much so that the very mention of the word can sometimes put people off (almost as much as the word 'ideation'). However, as long as the collaboration efforts are purposeful, with consideration given to structure, psychological safety and involvement, most groups will find brainstorming activities – of which there are hundreds of types and approaches – incredibly useful.

With so many more of us now working remotely, digital tools have really helped to bridge geographic and functional divides, fostering collaboration, both in real time and asynchronously. These include tools such as Mural and Miro for visual collaboration, Zoom, Teams and Slack for communication, or Trello for task management and prioritisation.

Fundamentally, though, trust building is the precondition to effective teamwork – and therefore collaboration.

In a professional environment, if I ask a group of people about teamwork – and what makes a team perform to a high standard, they may mention the name Lencioni. Patrick Lencioni's five dysfunctions form a pyramid or stack and, much like a house of cards, the order is important.[100] You need the bottom level to be in place before progressing to the next level.

In workshops, I often provide people with the five dysfunctions in a random order and ask them to put them into the right sequence, starting from the bottom. Try this now. In no particular order, the five dysfunctions of a team are:

- (Avoidance of) Accountability

- (Inattention to) Results

- (Lack of) Commitment

- (Lack of) Trust

- (Fear of) Conflict

Even people who are familiar with Lencioni's work often get this wrong, so when I subsequently reveal the correct sequence, they are surprised.

For teams to perform effectively, you require, in order:

1. **Trust**: Vulnerability and openness are the norm in your team.

2. **Conflict**: Your team is comfortable engaging in unfiltered discussion around important topics.

3. **Commitment**: Your team is able to buy into clear decisions, leaving little room for ambiguity and second-guessing.

4. **Accountability**: Your team members do not hesitate to confront one another about performance and behavioural concerns.

5. **Results**: Your team values collective outcomes more than individual recognition and attainment of status.

Of course, someone usually comments along these lines: 'Charlie, that's all very well, but I can't just walk in and ask my team to trust me.'

It's a fair point.

EXERCISE: Trust

Since the 2020 COVID pandemic, there has been a shift to more interactions happening online. I've heard many leaders at all levels say that rapport and trust are far more absent now than they were pre-pandemic. When I facilitate team-based sessions in person, regardless of the topic or situation, the attendees *always* comment on how much benefit they have felt by simply being together in the flesh. We are, after all, social animals.

Think about a current situation you're in, at work or in life, involving other people (eg work colleagues, team mates). How much do you really trust each other? If a significant mistake or ethical dilemma arose, do you believe everyone would be completely honest with you, even if it made them look bad or put them at risk? Would you feel completely comfortable leaving confidential information in their hands or asking them to handle a sensitive issue on your behalf? What hesitations, if any, come to mind?

This is why I use a version of Lencioni's model adopted by the military. It focuses in on what underpins the all-important trust, which helps leaders better understand what it is they need to do – or not do – to build that trust.

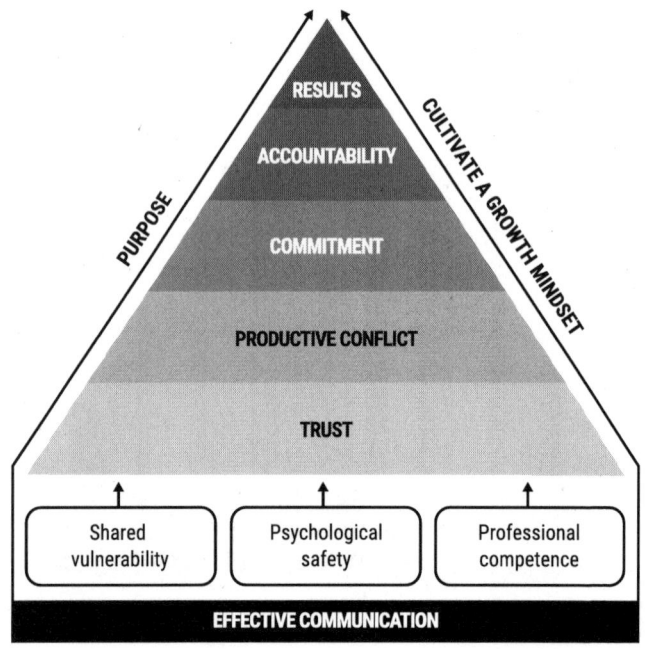

*Effective communication pyramid: adapted
from an interpretation shared by a military colleague
and used with permission*

As you can see here, below trust we have three
elements:

- Psychological safety – as explained in Chapter 6.

- Professional competence – think capabilities and
  behaviours, and the human iceberg. Just be aware
  of the Dunning Kruger effect – a cognitive bias that
  causes people to overestimate their own abilities,
  particularly where they lack knowledge or skill.

- Shared vulnerability.

Below all that? Effective communication.

That takes us right back to deepening self-awareness at the start of the strategic mastery framework – and again helps to explain why it is arranged the way it is. It also points us neatly to the final chapter – and the final practice of a strategist – influence effortlessly.

Why is communication so hard?

Eminent salesman Zig Ziglar is often quoted as saying that 85% of our success comes from our ability to deal with people, ie our relational skills – how well we know and interact with others. (This is often attributed to Dale Carnegie too, amongst others.) While the exact figure is difficult to verify, it captures the widely accepted truth that interpersonal abilities are central to professional and personal achievement.

These are the skills we often take for granted. We don't consciously focus on improving and developing them.

Imagine we are talking to each other. Between…

- What I am thinking

- What I want to say

- What I think I'm saying

- What I really say

- What you want to hear

- What you really hear

- What you think you understand

- What you want to understand

- What you really understand

… there are at least nine possibilities for mis-communication.[101]

For anyone in a leadership role who is reading this and scratching their head at the communication challenge, have a look at the trust wheel image below.

YOU SHOULD
Place more trust
in your people

THEY WILL
Be more motivated
to improve, develop
and learn

YOU SHOULD
Take (small) risks
on them

YOU SHOULD
Encourage them
to feel empowered
to act

**THE ROLE
OF TRUST IN
LEADERSHIP**

YOU SHOULD
Encourage them
to feel empowered
to act

THEY WILL
Feel directly
responsible for the
results

THEY WILL
Take on more
accountability

The role of trust in leadership

Many leaders look at this and instinctively say, 'Yeah, I do that', before noticing the direction of the arrows. 'Oh, hang on.' Acting in that direction is hard for leaders to do, but trust starts with you. Some argue that trust being earned, alongside command and control style leadership, is an outdated mindset.

A client was adamant that they were an exceptional leader (which they were in many respects) and had created high levels of trust – and performance – in their team. Had they ever asked the team about that? No.

It turned out that though their intentions were good and they would initially trust others with autonomy to get things done, and done to a good standard, this typically lasted less than an hour. Then they would dive back in and manage. You can probably draw on your own experiences of this happening to you – and how it feels – and how your behaviour adapts accordingly.

Let's finish with a short story on what can go wrong when communication and trust are not present from the highest levels of an organisation.

A STORY ABOUT RUMOURS

A friend of mine, who works for a major corporation, told me how a member of the executive leadership team passed him in the corridor and, rather catching him by surprise, stopped and expressed how sad they were to hear he was leaving the organisation.

'I'm not leaving!' he responded, somewhat alarmed.

'Oh, I'm sorry,' they replied, 'I must have the wrong person', and marched off.

You can imagine how unsettled he was – and for how long.

Don't allow a situation like the one above – or the apparent indifference of this senior leader – to arise in your organisation.

Actions

- **Set goals:** Define what strategic outcomes you want from your collaborative efforts. Make sure everyone understands the why behind being asked to come together. Sounds obvious, but this is so often missing.

- **Team audit**: Who's missing from your strategic conversations? Who else might you wish to invite? Whose perspective is missing? Intentionally invite people with different expertise and thinking styles to enrich the conversation and avoid groupthink.

- **Trust check**: Explore your team's views and opinions (anonymously) on what builds and potentially diminishes trust. What conversations are missing?

- **Understand motivations**:[102] Explore Kahler's Drivers, a tool that helps reveal the underlying needs and motivations behind your own and others' behaviours, especially in interpersonal situations. For example, are you someone who tends to please others? If so, how might that tendency limit your impact?

- **Talk time equity**: In your next meeting or conversation, ensure more balanced contributions. Use data to inform your collaboration efforts, collecting and reviewing metrics such as participation rates or decision quality to guide improvements.

- **Co-create**: Identify an opportunity to plan and facilitate a co-creation workshop or event, solving a real issue with cross-functional voices. Be bold and invite those you wouldn't normally involve, let alone consider.

- **Acknowledge collaboration**: Find ways to (publicly) acknowledge and appreciate an individual's contribution to collective success – and learn from their insights and experiences.

Key takeaways

- Collaboration enhances strategy and innovation. Diverse perspectives fuel creativity and lead to more effective human-centred strategic outcomes.

- Effective collaboration requires clarity. Without clear direction and roles, collaboration can lead to confusion rather than progress.

- Strategic collaborators build trust and inclusion. Good strategists foster psychological safety, actively listen and make space for diverse voices.

- Conflict, when managed well, is a source of creativity. It can stimulate deeper thinking and better solutions when approached constructively.

- Collaboration is a strategic skill. It demands intentional effort, the right mindset, and consistent behaviours to influence, align teams and drive results.

Remember Billie? Billie delights in collaboration, proudly calling it her superpower, because she knows true strategy doesn't happen in isolation. She loves to hear the perspectives of a wide range of people in both her business and her personal life – the more diverse, the better – and has learned so much from other ideas and cultures. Billie and her team work in perfect alignment, listening deeply as well as sharing their own ideas to come to agreements they are all clear on. Co-creation is something Billie values highly and she constantly hones the skills she needs to do it to the best of her ability.

Trust is paramount in Billie's team, and in her personal life. With this trust in place, she manages conflict well and turns it from a potential powder keg to an opportunity for creativity.

www.teammandarin.com/
resources/bemorestrategic

11

Be (More) Persuasive, Be An Influencer

You could be the best strategist and have the best strategy in the world, but if you can't get others on board, it is surely pointless.

As we've explored in previous chapters, being a truly effective communicator enables almost everything else to happen. I've coached thousands of people on areas of strategy and communication over the years, and have noticed that client organisations often ask me to home in on two particular subjects when we're designing bespoke development programmes: critical thinking and influential communications.

Initially, I was curious as to why these two unusual bedfellows were being paired, and how best to make them work together. However, as I started to facilitate the respective programmes, I realised that they are two sides of the same coin.

If being a good critical thinker is about being objective, logical, evidence based – and as a consequence, less easy to sway, persuade or potentially manipulate (without a clear, coherent and compelling fact-based argument) – then being a good influencer is about using many of the same skills. It's simply to your own benefit when you're the one presenting an argument to others and doing the persuading.

To do that really well requires practice, and builds on many of the skills and behaviours outlined in the earlier chapters. For example, identifying and understanding not just who your target audience is, but how their concerns, needs and motivations may be changing over time; foreseeing the potential implications and consequences of your suggested recommendation or action for that audience; distilling your thinking into a clear, coherent argument (an idea, a strategy, a proposal etc) and communicating that argument effectively with clarity and conviction, with authenticity, and – depending on the context – succinctly.

What is influence?

Influence is a word we hear every day, especially applied to social media, but what does it actually mean?

The Oxford Dictionary of English tells us that as a noun, influence is 'the capacity to have an effect on the character, development, or behaviour of someone or something, or the effect itself'. The *Merriam-Webster* dictionary defines influence as 'the power or capacity of causing an effect in indirect or intangible ways', and goes on to use the word 'sway'. In a professional context, especially if we're in leadership positions, it's useful to highlight the word 'power' here, ie having the power or power potential to cause an effect and do so without directly forcing it to happen.

If you explore the meaning and practice of influence in the business world, you will quickly stumble upon the seminal work of Robert B Cialdini, Professor of Psychology at Arizona State University, who wrote *Influence: The psychology of persuasion* back in 1984.[103] Interestingly, in various interviews, Cialdini has spoken about how the inspiration for the work that preceded the book was shaped by his early personal experiences.[104] This includes how, during his university days, he unexpectedly found himself buying a magazine subscription he hadn't planned on (*Sports Illustrated*), a seemingly mundane moment that sparked his lifelong curiosity about persuasive techniques and how easily our choices can be influenced. I'll come back to this point in a moment.

Cialdini blended personal stories with scientific insights in a way that has since become common in business and the behavioural science genre. In fact, he arguably paved the way for a whole category of books that I've inhaled over the last twenty+ years.

Relating Cialdini's work to some of the themes explored in this book, I've always appreciated the stories about how he immersed himself in the world he was seeking to better understand (we discussed immersion in Chapter 3). For example, he accompanied door-to-door salespeople on their rounds and even went undercover.

Principles of persuasion

From this work, Cialdini defined and developed six core principles that underpin any persuasive campaign:

- **Scarcity** – emphasise limited availability

- **Authority** – cite credible experts

- **Social proof** – show others are doing it

- **Liking** – build personal rapport

- **Reciprocation** – give something small first

- **Commitment and consistency** – encourage public or internal consistency

Cialdini later reflected that his experience with the magazine salesman exemplified the first three of these principles, all in just a matter of seconds while standing in Cialdini's doorway:

- **Scarcity**: This magazine was a limited resource that others (apparently) wanted. The salesman made his buyer (Cialdini) feel a sense of fear that he might be about to lose an opportunity.

- **Authority**: He cited the experts who'd read the magazine already.

- **Social proof**: He offered evidence that 'people like you' (Cialdini's fellow students) were buying the magazine.

All three of these remain foundational tactics today.

The remaining three are equally powerful. We are more likely to agree to someone's ideas and suggestions if we warm to them personally. This might seem obvious, but do people really think this through, even almost half a century later? Reflecting on my own work while looking at what's happening in the public domain (particularly today's politicians), I conclude that many people clearly fail to put this principle into practice.

Interestingly, in many high-performing teams and environments, you will hear – and experience – the concept of rapport before results. This is ultimately about how well we really know and trust each other. As highlighted by Patrick Lencioni's model in the previous chapter, with an absence of trust, teams will always struggle to improve their performance.

Reciprocation is about small favours paying great dividends. This was famously demonstrated by the psychologist Dennis Regan in 1971 in what became known as his Coca-Cola experiment.[105] Participants carried out a (meaningless) task in his laboratory one by one, and he would buy some of them a bottle of Coca-Cola. When the experiment was (allegedly) over, he asked the participants to buy raffle tickets for something he was personally involved in. He discovered that his prior behaviour (whether or not he'd bought someone a drink) significantly impacted their decision to buy. Those who'd received a bottle of Coca-Cola tended to buy not just one ticket, but significant numbers.

Commitment and consistency are best demonstrated by what happens if you ask someone whether they're going to vote in an election. Simply answering yes to the question will increase the chances of them casting a vote. Why? Because failure to do so would seem inconsistent and create an uncomfortable feeling of cognitive dissonance – of not acting in line with the person's values.

As Cialdini explains, 'Once we have made a choice or taken a stand, we will encounter personal and interpersonal pressures to behave consistently with that commitment.'[106]

EXERCISE: Influence drill

Step 1: Identify the situation.

Choose a situation where you want to be more influential (eg persuading a colleague, getting buy-in for an idea, increasing sales).

Step 2: Self-assessment.

For each principle, rate yourself 1–5 (1 = not using it, 5 = fully leveraging it).

- **Scarcity**: Do you highlight unique benefits or limited availability?
- **Authority**: Do you demonstrate expertise, credentials or experience?
- **Social proof**: Do you show that others are doing or supporting your idea/suggestion/proposal etc?
- **Liking**: Do you build rapport and find common ground?
- **Reciprocation**: Do you offer value first (help, advice, favours)?
- **Commitment and consistency**: Do you encourage small commitments leading to bigger ones?

Step 3: Take action.

Choose one low-rated principle – just one at a time – and come up with three potential actions to improve your use of it. Commit to act on them.

Example: if social proof is low, gather testimonials or show past successes. If authority is weak, highlight credentials or share expert opinions.

Implement the changes and observe the impact.

Influencing others

How much of your time do you spend influencing others in a typical working day or week? Probably a lot more than you think. Look through your diary, identify examples of when you were influencing, and reflect on what you were actually doing – and why – in those meetings, presentations, conversations and so on.

If you track it – historically and ongoing – you will become clearer on what you define as influence – beyond other awareness-raising benefits to doing this, for example the number, type and value of decisions, conversations, meetings, pitches you're involved in... any activities, really.

In Dan Pink's book *To Sell Is Human*,[107] he cites a figure of 40%+ for working professionals regarding the amount of time they spend influencing. Importantly, that's in non-sales roles. Having asked many people to think about this through my work, I believe the figure still holds.

Analysing your stakeholders

Stakeholder analysis is a rather dry-sounding approach taken from the world of project management. I remember learning how to do this as a young graduate. Although the approach is largely the same, the principles and disciplines of how to use this in a far more strategic way weren't mentioned at all.

In my mid- to late-twenties, I dusted off those notes while working with a major retailer on an innovative strategy – one that went on not only to win awards, but also to change the course of that business as a whole (it continues to be extremely successful).

In the early stages of the project, working as part of a core team of both internal staff and external experts,

I was tasked with thinking through our engagement plan and approach – identifying who all the business's stakeholders really were, from the obvious to the far less so, internally and externally, today and potentially in the future. This was important as the implications of the work could transform huge areas of the business and the wider ecosystem.

What became apparent, especially as the weeks passed by and momentum built, was just how important this role – and the supporting tools and conversation aids – would be. Many years later, I look to upskill people in knowing not just how to perform a stakeholder analysis properly, but how to make it part of a far more strategic approach and mindset for them and their team.

No one would argue that understanding your stakeholders isn't important, but people often bypass this step. I really don't know why.

Let's imagine that you're about to start a new project or initiative – or maybe you're partway through an existing one. All of your actions will potentially impact other people – maybe not immediately, but at some point in the future. I like to think of this like ripples on the surface of a still pond or lake.

You ideally need to know who all those people are *before* you act, or certainly before the ripples hit them. You are more likely to succeed with your project – in its entirety – if you have their support or, at a minimum, have pre-prepared your response.

A strategic stakeholder analysis should be performed project by project, initiative by initiative, with at least one other person. So many of the benefits lie – as with other strategy tools – in the conversations that are sparked by the correct use of the analysis.

Time and time again, I see the same pattern. Even if you're not currently performing the stakeholder analysis process, you might wish to reflect on these questions. Are you spending too much time with people who don't matter (in respect to the outcomes you're aspiring to achieve or the impact you're looking to have)? As a result, are you not spending anywhere near enough time – if any at all – with the people who do?

Considering consequences

We explored causes of problem solving in Chapter 5 on critical thinking. Now let's turn our attention to consequences.

Have you ever been a little nervous about sharing an idea, a proposal or a recommendation – maybe in a professional context (eg with a customer or supplier), maybe in your personal life (eg with a neighbour or friend)? When the moment comes to actually share that thought aloud, thirty seconds in, they stop you in your tracks, cutting you off mid-sentence and asking you about something that you recognise as being an excellent point – but it's one you've not considered at all. Their sentence often starts with, 'What if...?' or 'What about...?'

This can easily happen when you haven't spent enough time thinking through all the potential consequences of your proposal or plan, how it might play out and alternative scenarios, your Plan B, C, Z etc. All the people who reassured you by saying, 'Don't worry, I'm sure it will be fine, you're probably overthinking things...' are proved wrong in that moment.

Just to clarify, the good practice of reflecting, contemplating or thinking ahead to identify likely consequences should *not* be confused with overthinking.

EXERCISE: The value in asking 'So what?'

Ask yourself these questions *before* you share your recommendations:

- What new problems might be created by your recommendation, plan or solution?
- What are the potential implications? For whom?
- What will be the symptoms of those problems and implications?

Even a few minutes reflecting on these questions, perhaps exploring them with a friend or colleague, will ensure you're more on the front foot and optimise your chances of successfully influencing the audience and the outcome.

You may remember Sakichi Toyoda's 5 Whys from the Critical Thinking chapter. Let me introduce its lesser-known sibling – the 7 So Whats. Repeatedly ask yourself 'So what?' looking to outline or define the (potential) consequences of your (proposed) action. This is easier if someone else actually asks you 'So what?'

This is surprisingly challenging, but it will make you better prepared.

Many people miss opportunities for useful feedback by only asking friendly voices (sometimes called blue teams) to help them prepare for pitches, difficult conversations and so on. Try forming a red team too. This team will act more unpredictably – they might appear distracted, they might be late for meetings, they might cut you off, ask you to hurry up or start again. They will certainly ask 'So what?' and spot assumptions you're making or gaps in your argument.

This process is useful so long as the scope and expectations are set and you protect time to reflect and learn together afterwards. You also need to rotate the roles – you learn a lot by doing this from different positions (eg someone else shares what you're planning/proposing – and you get to respond as part of a red or blue team). You'll be amazed by your own creativity.

Distilling your argument

In a nutshell, keep it simple.

I'll paraphrase Steve Jobs: it takes a lot of hard work to make something simple, to truly understand the underlying challenges and come up with elegant solutions.[108] That's particularly true in communicating strategy-related concepts and ideas in a world awash with jargon.

One of the best books I bought in my early career was Barbara Minto's brilliant *The Pyramid Principle*.[109] I still use it for structuring narratives. Minto's principle is that most messages should have only one governing thought – the what. In communicating an argument, you must start from the apex of the pyramid, the governing thought or the what, which is held up by the lower levels of the pyramid, the supporting thoughts (the why) underpinned by facts and data.

This approach is intended for creating a presentation or report at the end of a project, but it's really useful to do this at the start too – helping you validate your thinking and spot flaws and gaps in your logic more easily to develop an argument flow. I first used the term 'argument flow' during my time at The Foundation, working closely with the founder and managing partner, the humble yet brilliant Charlie Dawson. Argument flow is a persuasive and actionable distillation of a large amount of information.

We would distil not only the information and insight, but also thoughts, instincts and feelings into a short, succinct strategic narrative or storyboard. We would do this mid-project (eg in the development of a new strategy or customer proposition) to test our own thinking (eg the logic or rationale, checking for gaps or blindspots etc), and share the emerging story with others for similar reasons.

One of our advisors, a journalist of high standing in the financial world, needed to be able to create a compelling argument of circa 500 words every day of the week to reflect what was happening in the world's financial markets – and share this in a way that was both insightful and engaging for the reader. He gave us the idea of identifying 'rocks' to stand on.

These rocks are facts that you know to be true. They are undeniable – however painful they are to hear or accept. In any conversation or presentation, you can always come back to them as your foundation, then build from there.

CREATING AN ARGUMENT FLOW

A few years ago, I ran a multi-day off-site strategy meeting for an organisation in Europe. At the end of the third and final day, the room was awash with flip charts and sticky notes.

The CEO asked when I was heading home.

'Tomorrow morning, 10ish,' I replied.

'Ah great. Would you like to have dinner with us this evening?'

'I'd love to – thank you.'

He gave me the details of time and location. Before he left, he turned to me and asked if I could do him one more favour.

'We have a meeting with our chairman at 9am tomorrow – any chance you could make sense of all this before then, and join us on the call?'

I now had to choose between three options. I could lie on the floor and go to sleep – which is what I felt like doing. I could say yes to his second question, accepting that I would have to miss dinner as I diligently captured and distilled everything that had taken place in the room over the last three days. I could say yes to both questions, knowing that if I trusted my ability to create a simple argument flow, I could do that in twenty minutes, take a few photos, pack up the room and join the CEO and his team for dinner with time to spare.

I opened a new document, set a timer for ten minutes and wrote five headers:

- What is the problem?
- Where is the problem?
- Why does it exist?
- What could we do?
- What should we do?

I then distilled these down to three headers: Issue (questions one to three), Insight (question four), Idea (question five).

I started on the left – the issue – and worked my way through the first three questions as I scribbled. Framing the issue clearly and concisely was the hardest part, but it became easier when I realised that there were two distinct issues – one more internally focused (ie about the organisation), the other more externally focused (about changes outside the organisation's immediate control or influence).

I made sure I had clear answers to the first three questions and they worked well together. Finally, I moved across to the emerging solution – the easiest part of the process – as my ten-minute alarm went off.

I paused, read what I'd written and checked for congruence, obvious gaps, potential assumptions in the argument. I verified a few facts from the notes in the room, then I started again – this time writing everything out in more concrete terms until a pretty clear argument flow emerged.

'That,' I told myself, 'is enough to share with the chairman tomorrow morning.' I then left for dinner.

There are many ways you might structure a good argument flow – the one above being particularly simple, but swift. This is because all the options had been identified and potentially explored to some degree already. It was the equivalent to sharing with the chairman five to six strategic options or pathways that the leadership team had prioritised and explored in that workshop.

'What could we do?' was the insight and 'What should we do?' was what the team believed should happen next, the decision that should be taken, what path they should follow – based on the argument presented and the evidence available (while remaining aware of their assumptions). This would be the conclusion the leadership team had reached – the strategic choices they had made and what direction they believed the organisation should follow.

The chairman found this incredibly helpful. The team was able to update him on three days of discussion in just a few minutes – in a way that was clear, congruent and compelling.

Remember not to use an argument flow during the work as a final statement or fait accompli. In the example above, from my argument flow, I was able to create a succinct summary of a three-day meeting that was recognisable and made sense to the people who were there, and to the chairman who was not. It was simple and punchy. Imagine you're talking to an eleven-year-old and you won't go far wrong.

Being persuasive

Now that you've distilled your argument – and validated it with others, checking your logic, identifying gaps and potential blindspots – it's about making it more persuasive and applicable for your audience. Think of this like the closing statement by a barrister to a jury. It is pivotal to a trial. The barrister is reminding the jury of the case theory and how the burden of proof has been met – explicitly sticking to the facts and evidence.

Build on the argument flow you've created to weave in more emotion. Think of something that you believe would hook your audience. This might be a personal story or an eye-opening statistic.

Whatever you do, be authentic. If you feel that you're forcing the hook, it might be better to skip it and focus on making a compelling opening statement.

CEO, speaker and writer Nancy Duarte in her brilliant book *Resonate* talks about the narrative fluctuating between what is and what could be.[110] Repeat that process, building tension.

An alternative is to create a simple narrative along these lines:

- State the current situation (rational, factual)

- Explain why this must change (emotive, painful)

- Share the key insight (belief, uniqueness)

- Finally, the solution (idea, recommendation)

EXERCISE: PSBA

Think about the audience you're trying to persuade. Sketch out four headers: Problem, Solution, Benefits, Action. Draft a maximum of two sentences under each header.

> The benefits (for that audience) are often the hardest to write. The action is for the audience, or you and the audience together. Think call to action.
>
> If you have sixty minutes, you can be more detailed. The problem might require ten minutes, the solution twenty minutes and so on. If your available minutes become six, or even two, you can simply collapse the level of detail back to the one to two sentence version.
>
> Try this: take a plan or strategy that you're involved in and articulate it using the PSBA format – with no preparation. You may be pleasantly surprised as to what emerges – and it will show where you're less clear or lacking evidence.

Knowing your audience

Your next task involves thinking through how best to apply your persuasive argument to your particular target audience. Think back to your stakeholder analysis – who needs to know about your argument, and who needs to know sooner than others? The sequence of who learns what by when and why might form part of your own influencing strategy (eg let Person X know first, as they might be able to help you persuade Person Y).

Draw a simple table with three columns and four to six rows. In the left-hand column, make a note of three to five key stakeholders, ie those you believe need to know sooner rather than later. Remember – you must be able to name them.

Now imagine that you're seeing each of these people at some point this week to share your argument, present your idea, have that all-important conversation. As a result of that interaction (think intervention), what must each of these people be left knowing, thinking or feeling? Person X might need to know the nth level of detail, whereas Person Y does not. Person X might need to be left thinking you're the right person for the job and Person Y might need to be left feeling particularly excited about your proposal.

In the middle column make notes on what each person must know, think and feel. In the right-hand column, outline what each person *does not* need to be left knowing, thinking or feeling. This helps to you be more focused on the scope of your interaction – and what and how you prepare.

As the intervention approaches, ask three questions:

- What's the purpose of the intervention?

- What impact do you want to have?

- What would be useful to know and understand about the audience?

This third question is about exploring the 'So what?' factor from earlier in this chapter, helping you to see and better understand the situation from the audience's perspective. Imagine you're standing in the audience's shoes. This is a process to do with other people – ideally people who are involved in the project with you and know the context and the audience, or could imagine them.

From the position or stance of your chosen/target audience, consider these questions:

- What are your goals and ambitions?

- What are your priorities – and what's less important?

- What are your needs and motivations?

- What are you concerned about?

- What's your communication style?

Psychometric tools are useful here, even if you've never been profiled yourself. They get people to consider and understand that they are a certain type, so not everyone thinks and feels and sees the world – and communication – in the same way that you do. The Insights Profiles are a good example,[111] and *Surrounded by Idiots* by Thomas Erikson sums up the concept nicely.[112]

Cultural differences are, of course, part of this preparation. They have a potential impact on every aspect of your influence campaign. Think through how the audience's cultural norms potentially align or clash with your own. If you're thinking this through from an organisational point of view, bear in mind the complexities of national and regional cultures, as well as organisational.

For example, you live and work in New Delhi, your client is based in Northern Germany. Your company is owned by a Japanese conglomerate – and theirs by a French one. What might you need to consider?

For more information on understanding cultural dimensions, look into the work of Dutch social psychologist Geert Hofstede.[113]

Amongst much advice given to me over the years by the wonderful Dave McCormick, who knows a thing or two about communicating strategic messages, here are some pointers to think about before you commit:

- **Think**: What story does your audience want to hear?

- **Decide**: What story do you want to tell?

- **Clarify**: What's the one governing thought?

- **Prepare**: What's the most appropriate structure for your story?

- **Practise**: What's the impact of your story?

Influence is more about connecting than selling. Focus on connecting your ideas to what matters to your audience. Combine clarity, empathy and preparation with a dash of listening and some resilience, and you will communicate in a way that inspires action and builds trust.

Actions

- **Prepare with purpose:** Before any meeting or conversation, clarify your know, think, feel goals for your audience – whether desired or not. What essential knowledge, mindset shifts and emotions do you want or need to evoke? Which ones do you want to avoid? Being intentional here sets the foundation for being an effective influencer.

- **Identify the governing thought**: Think of a pitch, proposal or recommendation you need to share or present in the near future. Use Minto's Pyramid to structure your messages logically and in a compelling manner.

- **Ask 'So what?'**: Ensure you've identified all the potential consequences of your recommendation or proposal by continuously asking this question (ideally, seven times). Do this in preparation. If your audience can't quickly answer, 'Why does this matter to me?', your message is likely to fall flat.

- **Keep it simple**: Strip away complexity. Practise aloud with someone who is unfamiliar with the topic – possibly playing devil's advocate. Express your argument as if you'll be addressing an eleven- to twelve-year old (perhaps practise with an actual eleven- to twelve-year-old). Practising with a devil's advocate or a child helps reveal hidden jargon or gaps in logic.

- **Three-minute pitch**: Craft a simple pitch for a current idea and recommendation using emotion, structure and clarity. Limit it to just three minutes.

- **Anticipate objections**: List and pre-empt three possible challenges to your argument. Practise with someone who is deliberately acting as the red team to rigorously test your arguments. Being prepared builds confidence and makes your message more robust.

Key takeaways

- Influence is strategic communication in action. Influence builds over time through trust, credibility and consistent reinforcement.

- Clarity drives alignment. Simple, structured messages are easier to understand and more likely to influence; complexity creates confusion.

- Effective communication is audience-focused. Tailor your message with a clear purpose and a defined impact in mind (know, think, feel).

- Anticipate and address resistance. Great influencers prepare emotionally and strategically to overcome objections before they arise.

- Emotion leads; logic follows. Stories persuade more powerfully than facts alone. Humans connect first with emotion, then reason.

Remember Billie? Everyone who knows her admires the way Billie effortlessly influences those around her, both socially and at work. Her proposals are met with enthusiasm and her ideas unite rather than divide groups and teams.

What Billie's friends, family and colleagues may not know is how much time and effort she has put into honing her skills as an influencer. She makes sure to know exactly who her ideas might impact, looking for even the most unexpected stakeholders and involving them in the conversation well before that impact is felt. She examines all the potential consequences of her proposals, to the point that 'So what?' becomes her favourite question.

Billie knows the importance of clarity when sharing a plan or proposal with other stakeholders. To that end, she keeps her presentations as succinct as possible, using argument flows to distil the pertinent points and keep everyone informed at regular intervals. She always considers the wants and needs of her audience, tailoring her arguments to each stakeholder so everyone gets what they need.

Billie has the skills and uses the practices of an exemplary strategist. As a result, she enjoys a happy, successful and fulfilling life.

www.teammandarin.com/
resources/bemorestrategic

Conclusion

A s we close this book, take a moment to reflect on how far you've come. *Be More Strategic* isn't just a book – it is a journey into the mindset, habits and behaviours that define truly impactful leadership. Whether you're leading a business, a team, a project – or simply aiming to lead yourself better – you now hold the tools to do it more strategically, more confidently and with greater purpose.

We began with the cornerstone of strategic leadership: self-awareness. You learned that effective strategy starts within. By tuning into your values, motivations and patterns of thinking, you gained insight into how your inner world shapes your outer actions. You discovered how reflection and emotional regulation can help you make decisions that are aligned, intentional and impactful.

From there, we moved to curiosity and open-mindedness – the superpowers of every great strategist. You saw how asking better questions, seeking alternative viewpoints and embracing ambiguity can open doors to innovation and smarter thinking. You learned that great leaders don't have all the answers – they ask the best questions and create the space for insight to emerge.

We explored the power of critical thinking – how to pause, zoom out and apply structured thinking to complex problems. You learned to challenge assumptions, weigh evidence and think more clearly under pressure. Alongside this came creativity, not as something whimsical, but as a disciplined practice that helps you imagine new possibilities, challenge norms and adapt in the face of change.

You developed strategies to navigate uncertainty, make bolder choices and take purposeful risks. We talked about being decisive – not reckless, but deliberate. You saw that collaboration and influence are essential to making your ideas stick. Strategy isn't a solo act. It's about connecting with others, building coalitions and moving people with you.

Perhaps most importantly, you learned that you can apply all of this in real life. You weren't just introduced to abstract theory – you were given frameworks, practical exercises and the relatable story of Billie, whose development mirrors your own. Strategy isn't reserved for the boardroom. It's for everyday leadership – for anyone ready to step up, think clearly and act with intent.

Your journey doesn't stop here. In fact, this is just the beginning.

Don't wait. Take everything you've learned here and turn it into bold action. The world needs more strategists. More leaders like you.

Now's your time. Let's go.

 www.teammandarin.com

Notes

1 ME Porter, 'What is strategy?', *Harvard Business Review* (1996), https://hbr.org/1996/11/what-is-strategy, accessed 24 July 2025

2 H Mintzberg, 'Strategy-making in three modes', *California Management Review* (1973), 16(2), https://cmr.berkeley.edu/1973/02/16-2-strategy-making-in-three-modes, accessed 24 July 2025

3 Sun Tzu, *The Art of War* (5BC) (Bibliotech Press, 2020)

4 RP Rumelt, *Good Strategy/Bad Strategy: The difference and why it matters* (Crown Business, 2011)

5 AG Lafley, RL Martin, *Playing to Win: How strategy really works* (Harvard Business Review Press, 2013)

6 R Martin, 'Decoding the strategy choice cascade' (Medium, 20 February 2023), https://rogermartin.medium.com/decoding-the-strategy-choice-cascade-475d40555eb1, accessed 14 May 2025

7 P Prakash, 'Airbnb's CEO says a $40 cereal box changed the course of the multibillion-dollar company' (Fortune, 19

April 2023), https://fortune.com/2023/04/19/airbnb-ceo-cereal-box-investors-changed-everything-billion-dollar-company, accessed 18 July 2025

8   M Gladwell, *Blink: The power of thinking without thinking* (Time Warner, 2005)

9   Inner Development Goals: Transformational skills for sustainable development, www.innerdevelopmentgoals.org, accessed 24 May 2025

10   R Martin, 'My eureka moment with strategy', *Harvard Business Review* (3 May 2010), https://hbr.org/2010/05/the-day-i-discovered-the-most, accessed 14 May 2025

11   A Kay, *Kay's Anatomy: A complete (and completely disgusting) guide to the human body* (Puffin, 2020)

12   D Goleman, *Emotional Intelligence: Why it can matter more than IQ* (Bantam, 1995)

13   ET Hall, *Beyond Culture* (Anchor Books, 1976)

14   C Dare, *Freud's Topographical Model of the Mind* (Routledge 1997)

15   A Gotter, medically reviewed by T Johnson, 'Box breathing: How to, benefits and tips' (Healthline, 2025), www.healthline.com/health/copd/box-breathing, accessed 24 May 2025

16   K Cherry, 'Biography of Abraham Maslow (1908–1970)' (Very Well Mind, 2025), www.verywellmind.com/biography-of-abraham-maslow-1908-1970-2795524, accessed 10 May 2025

17   C Dweck, *Mindset: The new psychology of success: How we can learn to fulfil our potential* (now called *Mindset: Changing the way you think to fulfil your potential*) (Random House, 2007)

18   N Shackleton-Jones, *How People Learn* (Kogan Page, 2019)

19   R Martin, 'What is strategic thinking' (Medium, 17 July 2023), https://rogermartin.medium.com/what-is-strategic-thinking-b0173112bb3d, accessed 14 May 2025

20   B Carey, *How We Learn: The surprising truth about when, where, and why it happens* (Random House, 2015)

21   J Waitzkin, *The Art of Learning: An inner journey to optimal performance,* (Free Press, 2008)

22 Press Room, 'Sir Clive Woodward talks to Monex about the "DNA of a Champion"' (Monex, 16 June 2020), www.monexeurope.com/press-room/sir-clive-woodward-talk-to-monex-about-the-dna-of-a-champion, accessed 25 July 2025

23 S Nadella, *Hit Refresh: The quest to rediscover Microsoft's soul and imagine a better future for everyone* (William Collins, 2018)

24 M Valcour, '4 ways to become a better learner', *Harvard Business Review* (31 December 2015), https://hbr.org/2015/12/4-ways-to-become-a-better-learner, accessed 14 May 2025

25 DH Pink, *Drive: The surprising truth about what motivates us* (Riverhead Books, 2009)

26 C Dweck, *Mindset: The New Psychology of Success* (Random House, 2007)

27 Dr N Velumyan, 'The silent superpower: How listening affects corporations' (Forbes Coaches Council series, 2025), www.forbes.com/councils/forbescoachescouncil/2025/02/11/the-silent-superpower-how-listening-affects-corporations, accessed 14 May 2025

28 C Drinko, PhD, 'We're worse at listening than we realize', *Psychology Today* (4 August 2021), www.psychologytoday.com/gb/blog/play-your-way-sane/202108/were-worse-at-listening-than-we-realize, accessed 14 May 2025

29 H Kawamichi et al, 'Perceiving active listening activates the reward system and improves the impression of relevant experiences', *Social Neuroscience* (2015), 10(1), 16–26, https://pubmed.ncbi.nlm.nih.gov/25188354, accessed 14 May 2025

30 N Kline, *Time to Think: Listening to ignite the human mind* (Cassell, 2002)

31 N Kline, 'The Ten Components' (Time To Think, 2020), www.timetothink.com/thinking-environment/the-ten-components, accessed 24 July 2025

32 SR Covey, *The 7 Habits of Highly Effective People: Powerful lessons in personal change* (Simon & Schuster, 2013)

33 SR Covey, *The 7 Habits of Highly Effective People: Powerful lessons in personal change* (Free Press, 1989)

34   CO Scharmer, *Theory U: Leading from the future as it emerges* (Berrett-Koehler Publishers, 2016)

35   M Russell, 'Strategic listening: The 3 levels of listening' (Medium, 27 November 2017), www.medium.com/swlh/strategic-leadership-the-3-levels-of-listening-e3f0c27f8d01, accessed 28 May 2025

36   R Martin, 'What is strategic thinking' (Medium, 17 July 2023), https://rogermartin.medium.com/what-is-strategic-thinking-b0173112bb3d, accessed 14 May 2025

37   R Martin, 'What is strategic thinking' (Medium, 17 July 2023), https://rogermartin.medium.com/what-is-strategic-thinking-b0173112bb3d, accessed 14 May 2025

38   UCL, 'What separates humans from AI? It's doubt' (16 April 2021), www.ucl.ac.uk/news/2021/apr/opinion-what-separates-humans-ai-its-doubt, accessed 28 May 2025

39   RA Heifetz, DL Laurie, 'The work of leadership', *Harvard Business Review* (December 2001), https://hbr.org/2001/12/the-work-of-leadership accessed 14 May 2025

40   Created in 1999 by Dave Snowden; described as a sense-making device. Cynefin is a Welsh word for 'habitat'. Detail taken from the Cynefin Framework website, https://thecynefin.co/about-us/about-cynefin-framework, accessed 14 May 2025

41   Air University, 'What is the RED Model of Critical Thinking?' (Edited 2019), www.airuniversity.af.edu, accessed 29 May 2025

42   J Liker, *The Toyota Way: 14 management principles from the world's greatest manufacturer* (McGraw-Hill, 2004)

43   W Buffett, 'Berkshire Hathaway Inc. Shareholder Letters' (1977–2024), www.berkshirehathaway.com/letters/letters.html, accessed 24 July 2025

44   G Hoffman, *Emotion by Design: Creative leadership lessons from a life at Nike* (Cornerstone Press, 2022)

45   J Silva, 'Flow lives at the intersection of discipline and surrender', (YouTube, 24 February 2020), www.youtube.com/watch?v=BmfTTXC0KW0, accessed 14 May 2025

46   M Oppezzo and DL Schwartz, 'Give your ideas some legs: The positive effect of walking on creative thinking', *Journal of Experimental Psychology* (2014), 40(4), 1142–1152, www.apa.org/pubs/journals/releases/xlm-a0036577.pdf, accessed 24 July 2025

47   K Matsumoto et al, 'The effect of brief stair climbing on divergent and convergent thinking', *Frontiers in Behavioral Neuroscience* (28 January 2022), https://pubmed.ncbi.nlm.nih.gov/35153696, accessed 24 July 2025

48   M Wong, 'Stanford study finds walking improves creativity', Stanford Report (24 April 2014), https://news.stanford.edu/stories/2014/04/walking-vs-sitting-042414, accessed 14 May 2025

49   R Martin, 'What would have to be true?' (Medium, 22 August 2022), https://rogermartin.medium.com/what-would-have-to-be-true-83dac5bd2189

50   J Galef, *The Scout Mindset: Why some people see things clearly and others don't* (Piatkus, 2021)

51   R Martin, 'My Eureka moment with strategy', *Harvard Business Review* (3 May 2010), https://hbr.org/2010/05/the-day-i-discovered-the-most, accessed 14 May 2025

52   B Stetka, 'Spark creativity with Thomas Edison's napping technique', *Scientific American* (9 December 2021), www.scientificamerican.com/article/thomas-edisons-naps-inspire-a-way-to-spark-your-own-creativity, accessed 24 July 2025

53   M Carr, 'How to dream like Salvador Dalí', *Psychology Today* (20 February 2015), www.psychologytoday.com/us/blog/dream-factory/201502/how-to-dream-like-salvador-dali, accessed 24 July 2025

54   C Jerome, 'Einstein at play', *Adirondack Life* (August 2016), www.adirondacklife.com/2016/06/28/einstein-at-play, accessed 24 July 2025

55   WT Gallwey, *The Inner Game of Tennis: The classic guide to the mental side of peak performance* (Random House, 1974)

56   DW MacKinnon, 'The nature and nurture of creative talent', *American Psychologist* (1962), 17(7), 484–495, https://awspntest.apa.org/doiLanding?doi=10.1037%2Fh0046541, accessed 14 May 2025

57   A Grant, 'The surprising habits of original thinkers' (YouTube, TED, February 2016), www.ted.com/talks/adam_grant_the_surprising_habits_of_original_thinkers, accessed 21 May 2025

58   T Urban, 'Why procrastinators procrastinate' (Wait But Why blog, 2013), https://waitbutwhy.com/2013/10/why-procrastinators-procrastinate.html, accessed 21 May 2025

59   P Skillman, 'The Design Challenge (also called Spaghetti Tower)' (Medium, 14 April 2019), www.medium.com/@peterskillman/the-design-challenge-also-called-spaghetti-tower-cda62685e15b, accessed 30 May 2025

60   P Kristiansen, R Rasmussen, *Building a Better Business Using the LEGO Serious Play Method* (Wiley, 2014)

61   A Grove, *Only the Paranoid Survive: How to exploit the crisis points that challenge every company and career* (Profile Books, 2022)

62   RS Lazarus, S Folkman, *Stress, Appraisal, and Coping* (Springer, 1984)

63   K Horney, *Our Inner Conflicts: A constructive theory of neurosis* (W. W. Norton & Company, 1993)

64   E Kübler-Ross, *On Death and Dying: What the dying have to teach doctors, nurses, clergy and their own families* (Macmillan, 1969)

65   Elizabeth Kübler-Ross Foundation, www.ekrfoundation.org/5-stages-of-grief/change-curve

66   E Berger (director), *Conclave* (Focus Features, 2024)

67   E Fox, *Switch Craft: The hidden power of mental agility* (HarperOne, 2022)

68   SR Covey, *The 7 Habits Of Highly Effective People: Powerful lessons in personal change* (Simon & Schuster, 2013)

69   K Weick, *Sensemaking in Organizations: Foundations for organizational science* (Sage, 1995)

70   Taoist Farmer Parable. Traditional Zen story, origin unknown. Widely retold in oral tradition and in modern interpretations of Eastern philosophy.

71   J Garvey Berger, *Unlocking Leadership Mindtraps: How to thrive in complexity* (Stanford Briefs, 2019)

72   JFK Presidential Library and Museum, www.jfklibrary.org/learn/about-jfk/historic-speeches/address-at-rice-university-on-the-nations-space-effort, accessed 21 May 2025

73   JFK Presidential Library and Museum, www.jfklibrary.org/learn/about-jfk/historic-speeches/address-to-joint-session-of-congress-may-25-1961, accessed 21 May 2025

74   R Martin, 'The Big Lie of Strategic Planning', *Harvard Business Review* (January 2014), https://hbr.org/2014/01/the-big-lie-of-strategic-planning, accessed 19 August 2025

75   'Broadband blues', *The Economist* (21 June 2021), www.economist.com/business/2001/06/21/broadband-blues, accessed 19 August 2025

76   S Brand, *The Clock of the Long Now: Time and responsibility* (Basic Books, 1999)

77   S Brand, 'Pace layering: How complex systems learn and keep learning' (JoDS, January 2018), https://jods.mitpress.mit.edu/pub/issue3-brand/release/2, accessed 21 May 2025

78   ME Porter, 'What is strategy?', *Harvard Business Review* (November–December 1996), https://hbr.org/1996/11/what-is-strategy, accessed 3 July 2025

79   M Lehman, *This High Man: The Life of Robert H. Goddard* (Farrar, Straus & Giroux, 1963) [later republished as *Rocket Pioneer* by Smithsonian Press]

80   A Madrigal, 'The day Goddard dreamed of taking a rocket to Mars', *The Atlantic* (19 October 2012), www.theatlantic.com/technology/archive/2012/10/the-day-goddard-dreamed-of-taking-a-rocket-to-mars/263856, accessed 24 July 2025

81   Robert H Goddard Papers, Robert Hutchings Goddard Library Volume I, Clark University Press (1898-1924), https://database.goddard.microsearch.net/Contents, accessed 4 July 2025

82   M Collins, *Carrying the Fire : An astronaut's journeys* (Pan, 2019)

83   Ibid

84   ME Porter, 'What is strategy?', *Harvard Business Review* (November–December 1996), https://hbr.org/1996/11/what-is-strategy, accessed 3 July 2025

85   I Pozin, 'One piece of advice from Mark Zuckerberg that will determine your success (or failure) in 2018', *Inc.* (19 February 2018), www.inc.com/ilya-pozin/one-piece-of-advice-from-mark-zuckerberg-that-will-determine-your-success-or-failure-in-2018.html, accessed 4 July 2025

86   B Casnocha, 'Reid Hoffman's two rules for strategy decisions', *Harvard Business Review* (5 March 2015), https://hbr.org/2015/03/reid-hoffmans-two-rules-for-strategy-decisions, accessed 21 May 2025

87   K Kruse, 'The 80/20 Rule And How It Can Change Your Life', *Forbes* (7 March 2016), www.forbes.com/sites/kevinkruse/2016/03/07/80-20-rule, accessed 19 August 2025

88   Amazon Staff, '2016 Letter to Shareholders' (Amazon, 17 April 2017), www.aboutamazon.com/news/company-news/2016-letter-to-shareholders, accessed 4 July 2025

89   R Coram, *Boyd: The fighter pilot who changed the art of war* (Little Brown & Company, 2002)

90   AJ Elliot, MA Church, 'A hierarchical model of approach and avoidance achievement motivation', *Journal of Personality and Social Psychology* (1997), 72(1), 218–232, https://doi.org/10.1037/0022-3514.72.1.218

91   E O'Donnell, 'The Third Way', *Harvard Magazine* (7 April 2021), www.harvardmagazine.com/2021/04/right-now-better-than-better, accessed 19 August 2025

92   'Wisdom of the crowd' is a well-established concept, originally popularised by James Surowiecki in his book *The Wisdom of Crowds* (Abacus, 2005)

93   M McKeown, *The Strategy Book: How to think and act strategically to deliver outstanding results* (Pearson Education Limited, 2012)

94 V Hunt et al, 'Diversity matters even more: The case for
    holistic impact', (McKinsey, 5 December 2023), www.
    mckinsey.com/featured-insights/diversity-and-inclusion/
    diversity-matters-even-more-the-case-for-holistic-impact,
    accessed 21 May 2025

95 E Larson, 'New research: Diversity + inclusion = better
    decision making at work' (*Forbes*, 21 September 2017),
    www.forbes.com/sites/eriklarson/2017/09/21/new-
    research-diversity-inclusion-better-decision-making-at-
    work, accessed 21 May 2025

96 'The first step: Langley's contributions to Apollo', (NASA,
    22 March 2019), www.nasa.gov/history/the-first-step-
    langleys-contributions-to-apollo, accessed 3 July 2025

97 Barrett Values Centre, website, www.valuescentre.com/
    resources#BarrettModel, accessed 21 May 2025

98 E de Bono, *Six Thinking Hats: Run better meetings, make faster
    decisions* (Penguin, 2016)

99 Interaction Design Foundation, 'What is design thinking
    (DT)?', www.interaction-design.org/literature/topics/
    design-thinking, accessed 2 June 2025

100 PM Lencioni, *The Five Dysfunctions of a Team: A leadership
    fable* (Jossey-Bass, 2002)

101 F Luntz, *Words That Work: It's not what you say, it's what
    people hear* (Hyperion, 2007)

102 T Kahler, PhD, 'Drivers: The key to the process of scripts',
    Transactional Analysis Bulletin (1975), 5(3), https://journals.
    sagepub.com/doi/10.1177/036215377500500318, accessed
    24 July 2025

103 R Cialdini, *Influence: The psychology of persuasion* (William
    Morrow, 1984)

104 S Vedantam, 'Persuasion: Part 2', Hidden Brain (23 January
    2023), https://hiddenbrain.org/podcast/persuasion-
    part-2, accessed 24 July 2025

105 DT Regan, 'Effects of a favor and liking on compliance',
    Journal of Experimental Social Psychology (November 1971),
    7(6), 627–639, https://doi.org/10.1016/0022-1031(71)90025-4

106   RB Cialdini, *Influence: Science and Practice* [4th edition] (2006 Pearson Education)

107   D Pink, *To Sell Is Human: The surprising truth about persuading, convincing, and influencing others* (Canongate Books, 2018)

108   W Isaacson, *Steve Jobs: A biography* (Simon & Schuster, 2011)

109   B Minto, *The Minto Pyramid Principle: Logic in writing, thinking, and problem solving* (Minto International, 1996)

110   N Duarte, *Resonate: Present visual stories that transform audiences* (Wiley, 2010)

111   Insights Discovery Profile, www.insights.com

112   T Erikson, *Surrounded by Idiots: The four types of human behaviour (or, how to understand those who cannot be understood)* (Vermillion, 2019)

113   The Culture Factor Group, website, www.hofstede-insights.com, accessed 21 May 2025

Acknowledgements

There are so many people who have influenced the writing of this book, but here are the ones that really matter.

Those I have worked closely with and those who have taught me what I know and understand over the last twenty+ years: Dave McCormick, Charlie Dawson, Steve Williams OBE, Simon Owen, Sam Roddick, John Sills, Ian Thwaites, Chris Allinson, Lisa McDowell, Arran Whitney, Greg Brown, the late Dr Tim Jones, Caroline Dewing, Patrick Harris, James Alexander OBE, Sara Milne Rowe, Ali Draycott, Katie Hodgson, Andrew Yeoman, Jack Milner, Dickie Farrelly, Lewis Moody OBE, Karen Callaghan, Helen Hatton, Tim White, Nigel Ford, Geoff Cousins, Andy Wolfe and Johnny Hammond.

Those who have inspired, coached and/or mentored me over that same time period, some possibly without realising the impact they've had: Peter Duffy, Simon Devonshire OBE, Simon Scott and most recently, Malcolm Doig.

Those who have helped this book become a reality: Matt Thomas, Shaa Wasmund OBE (and my amazing book writing cohort – you know who you are), Stuart Harris, Kerry Hopkins, Sophie Bratt. Plus all the original BETA readers: Andrew Yeoman (again), Jack Milner (again), Andy Bass, Ben Curson and Dan Colagiovanni. Plus the amazing members of my 'book club' who generously provided their time and feedback especially during the early stages of the book's development (and for some, right up to its completion): Chas Hallett, Simon Evans, Sandra Sloan, Sonal Ambasna, Kate Wilson, Catarina Cruz, Antonia Eyton-Jones, Anthea Bartram, Ben Murphy, Aleksandra Peribere, Michal Leszczynski, Dr Naomi Clemons, Ed Tyler, Greg Bull, Adrian Turner, Malgorzata Jermakowicz (MJ), Sheila Hines Edmondson, Michelle Bisset, Rachel Ferguson, Amy Bingham, Piotr Jankowski, Andrew Bose, Ben Hiard, Andy Waring, Chris Guest, Toby Burge, Julie Johnson, Helen Mee, Doug Rose, Shuja Khan, Alex Pond and Herwig Kusatz.

The team at Rethink, in particular Anke, Eve, Sarah, Geraldine, Joe and Alison.

Most importantly, I would like to thank all my clients and colleagues over the past twenty-five years, as working with you has been where so many of

the insights, learnings and stories in this book originated. I won't even attempt to name you all as I am
bound to forget someone incredibly important – but
a particular thank you to those who encouraged me
to write this book.

Finally, thank you to my amazing wife, Sally, and
beautiful children, Evie and Freddie, who all put up
with me going through this book writing process –
losing me to the shed at the bottom of the garden for
many months.

The Author

Charlie Curson is a strategic advisor, investor, facilitator and accredited leadership coach. With over twenty-five years of experience, Charlie has worked with more than 250 organisations across thirty+ industries – from global giants like VISA, McDonald's, Unilever, Experian, Volkswagen Group, L'Oréal and Barclays to ambitious start-ups – helping to design and deliver bold growth strategies, innovation programmes and leadership development initiatives.

A natural integrator of research and real-world application, Charlie blends cutting-edge theory with practical tools to support leaders, teams and organisations navigating uncertainty and change. He is an accredited Leadership Circle Profile coach, with thousands of hours of executive and team coaching experience, and is regularly called upon to facilitate global leadership programmes that focus on building strategic capability, adaptability and influence.

Charlie believes that being strategic is not just a skillset – it's a mindset. His work helps people and organisations unlock clarity, direction and momentum. He specialises in helping leaders become more conscious, more creative and more effective – in work and in life. Whether it's through coaching, advising or facilitating, his goal is to empower others to develop greater self-awareness, think strategically and act decisively with positive intent.

Described by clients as anything from a Swiss Army knife to a nexialist,[†] Charlie is passionate about simplifying the complex and enabling others to make meaningful, lasting impact. This book was written in response to years of client nudges – and is rooted in the same practical wisdom, hard-won insights and strategy and coaching frameworks he has shared with thousands to great effect around the world.

---

† A nexialist is someone who integrates insights from multiple disciplines (eg physics, astrology, sociology, economics etc) to solve problems and create innovative solutions. It might also be referred to as holistic problem solving or systems thinking. The term itself was coined by AE van Vogt, a Canadian science fiction writer, in the 1950 novel *The Voyage of the Space Beagle*. In the novel, the protagonist, Grosvenor, helps his crew navigate and survive extraterrestrial threats by applying his broad cross-disciplinary expertise, seeing patterns and connections that specialists in individual fields miss. Grosvenor is a nexialist.

Charlie is a keen but fairly average sportsman, runner, mountain biker and occasional DJ. Despite being a futurist and space geek, he still hasn't dabbled there professionally, but if you work in the space industry and have an opportunity, he would love you to get in touch.

Connect with Charlie:

🌐 www.teammandarin.com

in linkedin.com/in/charliecurson

⊙ @charliecurson

✉ hello@teammandarin.com